UNCLE TOM AT HOME.

UNCLE TOM AT HOME.

A REVIEW

OF THE

REVIEWERS AND REPUDIATORS

OF

UNCLE TOM'S CABIN BY MRS. STOWE.

BY F. C. ADAMS,

BOOKS FOR LIBRARIES PRESS
FREEPORT, NEW YORK

First Published 1853
Reprinted 1970

STANDARD BOOK NUMBER:
8369-5210-3

LIBRARY OF CONGRESS CATALOG CARD NUMBER:
78-107789

PRINTED IN THE UNITED STATES OF AMERICA

A REVIEW FROM HOME

IN ANSWER TO THE REVIEWERS AND REPUDIATORS

OF

𝔘𝔫𝔠𝔩𝔢 𝔗𝔬𝔪'𝔰 𝔠𝔞𝔟𝔦𝔫

BY MRS. HARRIET BEECHER STOWE.

BY

F. C. ADAMS.

Introduction.

WE have taken up the book upon its merits in answer to those who have preceded us upon its demerits.
We have viewed its spirit and intention at variance with
its violent adversaries, and we know there are many
good Southerners who do not differ with our opinions,
and who would fain see the cankering evil removed.
In their hands lies the remedy; and if they will but ap-
ply it, they can disarm their enemies. The point is
there; and while the many happy associations which
undoubtedly exist between master and servant should
be properly valued, the imperfections and miseries of
an institution, that weighs heavy in the balance of a
great country, should not be buried under their mantle.
There are many phases in the institution, and we shall
endeavour to give those phases impartially in a forth-
coming work. The Southerner knows, and acknow-
ledges the evil which is upon him—and if he will, he can
do more to stay the bad master's cruelty than all the
force of organised bodies at a distance. In our com-

parisons we have not wandered far away from the
homes of the reviewers who have preceded us, and
have only cited such instances as must be familiar to
them, and to which we have called the attention of our
brethern of the press, while at the south. We give
the facts with a knowledge that no fiction, however
great the scope of imagination may be, can out-glare
the reality in its dark phase, pictured by the Author.

F. C. ADAMS.

CHARLESTON, 1853.

Uncle Tom at Home.

A REVIEW TO THE REVIEWERS.

BY A SOUTHERNER.

———◆◆◆———

THAT book of books, that has passed the ordeal of all scribblers, from the lordly down to the penny-a-liner, still continues unharmed. It has afforded many themes for little genius, and great points for great men, who have poured out their vehemence against it only to give it greater pre-eminence. And now that Southern criticism has exhausted itself, ceased its struggles, and yielded its force to Northern champions, who out-southern Southerners in the front rank of the pro-slavery charge. From the sagacious political reviewer, who has heaped his vengeance upon its pilgrim head, it has passed to the more amiable *month-lies,* who have hitherto contented themselves with

(7)

pleasant musings, and governed their modesty to
please fair ladies. These latter, with Godey and
Graham's goodly numbers combined, have assumed
the sponsorship, and aspire to do for the South
what the South will not do for herself—uphold the
wrongs of slavery. Their motive is their own—
we shall pass it, and if their hopes be realized,
let us trust the recompense will be applied to a
good cause. Since it is so, we claim a right to
make a few remarks from a home source—a simple, comparative review, which can neither offend
nor injure a good cause.

But let us ask: why has South Carolina shown
such manifold earnestness in her rebukes against
a " Yankee Woman's" little book?   Her sensitive
chivalry seems shocked; the theory of her fortunes
is told; truth is uncomfortable, and her slave
philosophy quails beneath its influence.   Her
best panegyrists have come forth to preserve her
honour, disclosing the secret of making base spirits
noble, and with singularly potent and persuasive
sunny effusions, plead the intensity of love for
truth.   Are they sincere?

Poor " Uncle Tom," like a pilgrim on his weary
way, still continues through Christendom.   What

a lie-reading world this of ours must be, if Southern statements be true !

But if South Carolina criticism be true, why
not give it 'to us by a rule of consistency? not
by that vain flourish that would encircle wrong
with an excessive brightness, and make South Carolina the principality of the South.

The criminal trembles when truth is deposed
against him—so it is with those who oppose the
material subject of this book, reviewing it upon
technicalities instead of principle, and thus South
Carolina, more sickly than her sisters, calls loudest
for a physician.

The truth lays prostrate at her own door, and
her defenders make her wrongs right with the
beauty of abstractions, rather than acknowledge
the evil, and create justice the guardian of power.
The simple truth has found its way, amid her ham-
pered necessities, to the very fountain of material
wrong, kindling the inventive ambition of her va-
liant sons; and unblushing in that shame which
sets the moralist and philanthropist at defiance,
they come forward to the world to tell it of *pious*
slavery and its joys.

If slavery be full of joy and piety, why nurture

that spirit, so manifestly your own, that would plunge a dagger to the heart of him who dare speak *liberty* in your streets? These loud acclamations, "soundings of joy," "beauties of truth," and domestic homilies, cannot awaken the sympathy of common sense, much less the confidence of those who have been casual sojourners in the South.

But it may be asked, why do we take up the book?

We answer, because we have witnessed the manifest workings of that peculiar institution—seen the different phases of Southern life, and watched them in their changing attitudes. And while doing this, it was the fortune of our misfortunes to be placed where we could witness the misery, woe, suffering and brutality of the slave system. Yea— not only the miseries of the slave system itself, but the dissolute and degraded condition which it entailed upon the poor, labouring whites. The *primrose* of a name has done much for the South, and yet all is not substance that glitters there; the legends of her shaded bowers, vast plantations, noble hearted planters with *human* wealth in store, are things that have lived in a name and die in the shadow.

To South Carolina they are like the golden
dream of her Southern Congress, and *home* prized
equanimity—things lost in their own existence.
True generosity and hospitality have their founda-
tions at home; and it becomes us to inquire how
far we must credit the grandeur of those noble
characteristics to those who would starve a human
being at home—estrange the last stage of spent
life—measure his peck of corn with mathematical
exactness, and quibble over his task to sound a
name abroad.   Men who mount upon the higher
impulse of popular ascendency must maintain it
by justice and right; they must second their pro-
testations with the patriotism of justice in its moral and legal qualifications; they must first recognize the things that are around them, calling
for the good will of man to man.   The day has
passed when men could mount some high-born pin-
nacle, and sound their stentorious voices in behalf
of the moral grandeur of an institution, when its
hideous vices stared them in the face at every
turn.   Such soundings have become ineffectual,
their misconstructions too glaring, and the motive
too boldly outlined to need a delineator.   But we
will discuss these things in their proper places.

The vivid recollection of many happy associations at the South, the friendship we have met, the kindness of those who knew us through strange vicissitudes, and our well known position, constrains us to touch many things as lightly as possible, and to pay due deference to the fine-strung sensibilities of our brethren. We take up the subject of the book in admiration of its truthful delineation of a species of Southern life, and the spirit of its intention, to point those who have gone before us, especially W. Gilmore Simms, Esq., to facts which are seemingly overlooked. Let us *hope* it was not intentional, nor shared for the hope of gain or fame.

The question is, *the book;* the "Yankee Woman's" book—its truth or falsehood.

Christendom has passed judgment upon it, and South Carolina has repudiated it. Her chivalrous sons, from the poet and play-*writer* to the wayfaring scribbler, who throws his mite into the hopper to decorate the columns of "the *Courier*," have volunteered their energy, fervor and wisdom to thwart the influence of a "Yankee Woman's" little book. There is a fanciful pleasure in cherishing these domestic offsprings, harmless abroad,

and so in keeping with those spirit-burning toasts
at home, that they become the best and most valuable advertisements of the book. They carry
the feelings of a vigorous minority into the keen
senses of the distant observer, showing that the
truth must be strong against a selfish institution,
when so much fiery opposition is marshalled to
repel such a small messenger.

Many of these harmless, little flashes of the
brain are beneath criticism, for they neither im-
part character, regard truth, nor plead the honest
Southerner's cause.

Before we take up Mr. Simms' "Southern
view," we must give a passing notice of that
novel and particular point in a work—well di-
gested in South Carolina—entitled, "Slavery in
the Southern States," the accredited production
of a Mr. P ——, a member of the legal profession
in Charleston, claiming caste in the higher walk.

We will not charge Mr. P—— with want of
forbearance in his mission, nor lack of profound
devotion to his cause—for in these Mr. Simms
would have added consistency to his review had
he copied his moderation. But unfortunately for
the genius of Mr. P——, he has shown the com-

plex nature of his subject to be so great that he is troubled to find a beginning, and stop at the ending. Enjoining many good things upon an incurious and forbearing public, he seems to forget that in displaying the beauty of *amiable* weakness the object of the book is lost upon the mind of the general reader, and that which he intended for force is taken for speculation. The reader will ask us, What is Mr. P——'s object?

It is to prove that slavery enforces Christianity —in other words, that it is a divine transcendent. With his ascetic mode of reasoning, he has not classified the sources from which he has drawn his result, nor given us the difference between the established *morale* of true Christianity, and the Christianity of usage made to conserve obedience. Nor has he descended to the latent power which holds the absolute force and intention of his own involuntary Christianity. The Southerner tells you 'twere well to Christianize his property because of its value, and as a better means of subjection. At the same time he tells you the church is all humbug, and holding absolute power over the material object, he becomes the self-appointed apostle of its Christian virtues. According to Mr.

P——'s dictum the whole force of this species
of Christianity is dependent upon the moral character of the slaveholder; yet he has not given us
the quality of that morality, which, according to
his own arguments, is to become the great regulator of his divine institution.   We have no inclination to question the scale of morality with Southerners, nor its influence upon the slave, who, by
necessity, studies his master's nature, and frequently copies his vices ; but the proof against
Mr. P——'s doctrine is too deeply founded in
national sense to need any further strength of
argument.

Nor do we want their mathematical and metaphysical conclusions, because there is a more simple mode of testing them ; yet we are at a loss
to know how Mr. P——, with his own private
knowledge, could have arrived at such Christian
conclusions, unless he has fallen into those by-gone
errors of a forced theology, overlooking the truth
of practical results, illustrated at his own door.

In all our intercourse with Southerners, we
never heard one claim moral caste for the institution of slavery ; but not unfrequently have we
heard them denounce instances of outrage upon

chastity, sustained in the rights of the master, and beyond the remedy of laws made to govern the outraged. With our knowledge of social life in Charleston, we feel no hesitation in saying, that Mr. P——'s erudition in behalf of the divine precepts of slavery will prove as novel to Southern readers, as it will be forcible to those of more Northern sensibility. But the reader must remember that the quality, depth, and attributes of Christianity, according to the rule of progress, are at the present day measured by a scale of locality. That which is made the medium of an accommodating morality in Charleston, would be rejected as unwholesome by the sterner judgment of the New Englander.

Upon these considerations, we can be charitable with Mr. P——, and attribute his singular errors to the fact of having founded the sliding-scale of his Christian conclusions upon the texture of this species of morality—a morality opening a grand arena for the pleasures of those who wish to enjoy. It was fortunate for the author that his book came out at an unfortunate time, otherwise his reputation for literary pursuits would have reflected upon his legal abilities: yet there is nothing without

its consolation, and Mr. P—— has his in a knowledge of his book being a book *for home,* and not
for the critical observation of a reading public in
this enlightened age.   He has lost the medium
which enlists the confidence of the common reader,
in trying to bury the issue of natural law with the
beauties of his pen; a fault much in vogue by
those who consider themselves polished writers.

Had he traced the effect of a small minority
governing a majority, he would have qualified his
moral disclosures, and made a small exception for
those evils which must naturally arise from the force
of power necessary to subject one to the will of the
other.   Or if he had treasured his divine disco-
veries, contrasted them with the prospect of that
majority being held in an absolute and abject condition, subject to the good or bad traits of the
master's character—his positive will—changing
fortunes, and those unforeseen events which have
brought so many poor wretches into the hands of
tyrants, he would have added force and consistency to his book, strengthening the better division of his cause.   His efforts might have promised something in the future, instead of burdening his logic with the beauties of slave-life.   His

2

generosity would have had life, and he, with some
plausibility, claimed a hopeful diffusion of spiritual life for his slave, and made the common reader
believe there was truth in it.

Our object being to notice the book upon one
point only—the only one upon which it claims
attention, we shall give Mr. P—— a simple contrast, leaving the reader to draw his own conclusions.   It is a simple and singular process of testing Mr. P——'s logic, but having lived in his
own neighbourhood we will invite him to its standard of morality.

Will you go with us into the innumerable by-
ways of your "sunny city?"   They are lined with
little cottages, inhabited by semi-saxon females,
whose flaxen-headed children know a father—not
to recognise him as such, but to fear him.   We
will enter together !   The picture around us is
full of measured humbleness—shall we ask the
unhappy woman who prides in being the mistress
of a *gentleman*, who is her *"friend ?"*   No, we
will not ask her, for custom has made it a social
generality—*we know!*   Let us trace him to his
mansion, because they are things of common life.
He has a pretty family there, and they go to

church *every* Sunday.   Certainly! there's no getting over that—and papa goes *too*, puts on one
of the very best faces for Christian modesty, opens
the prayer book for dear wife, pats the little legitimates on the head, and reminds them of their
duty to the good parson's sermon.   While this
very necessary species of puritanism is manifest-
ing itself below, his pensive mistress sits in the
gallery, enjoying the sovereign contemplation of
her own feelings.   Around her, are those little,
interesting intermixtures, *doubted* and disowned,
peeking over the railing at " *daddy below*," like
as many ferrets motioning about a stone wall: but
they must not insinuate with their fingers.

There is a wide difference between the quantity
and quality of Christianity; and the latter should
be well judged before the former is credited.

We are treading on delicate ground; but must
invite Mr. P—— to go further with us, and be a
missionary among the specimens.

Which way will you go—east, west, north or
south?   We are now in the centre of the city,
and the course is immaterial.   The same prospect
is before us in every street, lane, and alley, and
on the *neck*.   Here are the demonstrators—you

know them, and you must not shut your eyes,
nor feel about for Christianity. Well! we'll
step into Old Ned Johnson's on the neck. It is
a miserable rookery, but an average sample of
those " *all around town*"—not excepting those
attached to several princely dwellings. Don't
stop at the door, because it " a'nt so neat as your
own little place." Sit down on that primitive
box by the fire-place. Yes, that's well; put your
handkerchief over it. "Ned don't keep things
the nicest," nor does " old Misses lef' um nuf to
hab' chare fo gemmen." Ned's simple story is a
counterpart of what could be told by thousands in
your city—at least, seven-tenths of the coloured
population of your city.

Ned is one of the cleverest "old niggers"
about; black as a crow, honest as *any nigger*,
" *for all niggers 'll steal*," and has always worked
just like a nigger. His wench, old Mumma, is
as motherly an old "thing" as you ever did see,
and a Christian at that. Yes, just as sound as a
nutmeg in her belief, and thinks she'll go to heaven just as "straight as white folks." You must
see her, and learn from her the very best original
ideas of Christianity; give ear to her simple

dialogue—and if you comprehend her logic, it may assist in propping up your new system of Christianity—founded upon the slave law. Ned will go and bring her in.

Three young imps, as "black as vengeance," half naked, and as dirty as wharf-rats, come scampering into the house—perfect pictures of Old Ned. They rumage about the house, and in the old basket where Ned keeps his "nigger fodder, " to find some corn cake. But da's nofin da', no corn to make im wid." Its scratching times with Ned; he's been laid up nearly a week with a lame arm, his time is running on, and that old widow A——m would grind his marrow bones for the wages.

You say :—" Well—we—know; there's a good many hard cases about town—and especially these foreigners that buy slaves to profit by their increase, selling their own children in the market. But—good Lord, it would'nt do to be everlastingly bothering yer head about the troubles between niggers and their masters. Its infernal unpopular; you'd get yourself into a pretty fix about town."

Ned has returned, and with an humble suavity,

informs us that Mumma "come fo' soon." She's got some work at fifty cents a day, which will help to pay old Misses for Ned's time. Let us ask Ned a few questions.

"How old are you, Ned?"

"Ha! hah!! ha-e!!! Why Massa, hard fo'h tell dat. Spose I's 'bout sixty som 'ow. Old Miss say 't'ant so by good pile. Lor, Ned know what Old Miss up to. Can't wuk no how, Massa, like when I out on old Massa plantation; old Miss know dat, 'but no' lef im gone; drive old Ned jus so yet."

"Where do you work, Ned?"

"I stows cotton on de waf; I'ze fus rate at dat; gets dollar and seven pence a day."

"How much a month do you give old Missis for your time—clear share?"

"Why Lor, Massa, dat 'quire some calatin. When old Massa lib' an I cumes down to wuk ater all done gone on plantation, den I pays old Massa twenty dollars ebey mont. Old Massa good old boss; when Ned did im up right, gin um dollar now and den!"

"We don't care about that; we want to know what you pay now!"

"Well, old Massa die—good old soul; you now'd him Mass P——, dat you did. Den Massa Genl. Hamilton cum cecutor ob de state : he no'd I 'warnt right, an 'e jus make old Miss content ersef wid sixteen dollars."

"Do you support your wife and family with the balance ?"

"Sartin—must do dat, an old Miss such straight Christian make Ned gib for'h dollars fo church ebe year. Old Miss look right sharp fo' cash. Put em-up in jail once, den send em to wokouse, and give em hinger cus lef wages run pass one week ! Lor, Massa, Old Ned seen some ard time in is life—tell you dat. But my old woman gals got fuss rate friends—*help some, old Miss know dat.*"

"Ah ! how's that ?   What's the difference between your children and her children ?"

"Whew ! mighty site massa, you know dat. *Don't* take no losopher what own slaves to reckon!"

"How long have you been married, Ned ?"

"Massa, jus long nuf 't hab dem tree," pointing to the woolly-headed imps who had huddled into the fire place.   "Old woman hab two '*bright gal*' fo I marry her !" he continues with emphasis.

O yes! she was a widow when you married her :—****.

"Massa, I sees yes green, 'aint liv souf long no how. Old Massa know all bout dem gal. He says gwine to lef 'em free when 'e die; but *Buckra* very unsartin, an 'e don know if 'e die wen he gwine to. Old Miss watch dat an put em fo'h true. Boff on em be *mighty likely gals.*"

"Well, Ned, where is Nancy now?"

"Lor, Massa, you knows; her friend keep big store on *de Bay* (street next the wharves). "Da 'ant no bigger geman den he bout town."

"Did he buy her from old Missis?"

"He did dat—gin her nine hundred dollar. Nancy got right smart boy now, jus as bright as you is, Massa."

"Misses always goes to church—does she Ned?"

"Yah! yah!! yah!!! she what do dat; neber hear church bell ring widout see old Misses gwine."

"Honest Christian! What a pleasure there is in faith," thought we.

"Did she ever sell you, Ned?"

"Old Missis get strange bout two year ater old Massa die, and sell me way down Christ Parish —get right good heap for me den. But lor, Massa, dey work nigger down da anyhow, and don't gin notin to eat nohow. It aint no way to make nigger wuk so. No bacon to grese 'e troat wid, and stick de lash to 'e back so! I mose dead in two years, and beg old Miss to buy me back, cos I warn't wuf much nohow."

"What did they feed you on, Ned, and what were your Christian principles?"

"Just what all Massa's gib nigger down yonder—peck corn every week—nofin else. Massa how I gwine to be Christian? No lef em read— no Church, and Massa Carl say work for sef on Sunday, get bacon. Massa take 'e dog an go hunt Sunday. Nigger work 'e own *patch* for get bacon and lasses. Mighty few planters what gib nigger bacon down Christ Parish."

"Could'nt you steal, Ned?"

"Why, Massa, jes foce to dat—do I warnt Christian. Buckra man say all nigger steal— spose I jes' well own him. But Massa, nigger don't steal wus den Buckra gin him same chance for nuff to eat. But 'e mighty dangerous business fo' nigger. We tefe Massa Genl. Quattlebum hog down swamp one night. Massa Genl. hear de sarpent squeal, an cum wid 'e gun. Whiz! ziz!!

ziz'!!! de way he shoot 'em wid 'e double barrel
mose kill Jef an me—den old Massa *buck* de
whole on us next mornin. Lor, I beg old Miss take
me back, so I see my old woman. Old Miss tink
sometime by-'n-bye feel like Christian an did em
straight. Iz a Christian now, Massa, an wanted
to be one den, but old Massa no lef em nohow."

Here comes old **Mumma**; a description of her
is unnecessary—we only want her simple experience in our author's theology. She has been a
hard worker in virtuous toil, and yet she struggles
to get the price of a corn cake and a little hominy.
Two beautiful "bright gals" follow her. They
are finely formed, with classic faces, features well
developed, and enlivened by the striking beauties
of Saxon birth. One seems a few years older
than the other—neither look like Mumma, and yet
they are hers. She's right glad to see us, but her
domicile is the index of poverty, and she feels con-
scious that she cannot receive us properly, But
we must know her experience.

"Mumma, what has made you a good Christian?"

"Don know dat?—Why, de Lord! dat jus as
sartin as Massa Buckra preach." * * * * * * *

"Well, Mumma, whose girls are these?"

" O, dem mine fa' true : hab dem long time ago. Old Massa high old boy den."

"And these little woolly-headed rascals—yours too, Mumma?"

"Jus so true—Ned know dat."

" Ah, Mumma !" * * * * * * *

" Why Lor, Massa, how I helf him? Old Massa own me den, an 'e lash 'e back ———."

" Were you a Christian then, Mumma?"

" P—s—h !! What you ax dat fo'? How I be Christian wen Massa no lef em! *Iz go for Church den.* Cus Massa say he best; and nigger alays like to! Áter Ned and I gets married fo' true den I jins de Church wid Ned—true Christian den !"

" Is your eldest daughter married, Mumma?"

" Why, Massa, she married jus like all bright gals.———Her friend buy her of old Missis long time ago. He rich geman—' *do well*' by her so far: God know Massa how long he last so; *Buckra* very unsartin in such tings. Just like 'e marry somebody, den send she to Old Massa Gadsden for sell—"   *   *   *   *

This is a simple mode of testing the quality of

Mr. P——'s specific theology; but we must proceed a little further.

"Does she go to church, Mumma?"

"I would'nt be dat gal if she didn't go to church—neber miss em. She just de Christian what 'Buckra man' make her."

"About this other one, Mumma—Christian too?"

"Why, Massa, what make 'e ax sich questions— ye 'ant parson nohow:—Her 'friend' fus rate geman—but im done want nofin said bout it cos he jine de church 'e sef. Old Misses know it sartin fo true."

"Does Old Misses own her yet?"

"Lor, yes! Dat gal pay Old Miss four dollar ebe week—*clare at dat.*"

"There's no doubt of Old Missis being a good Christian?"

"Massa, you know Old Miss; she's jist the straifist Christian ye ever seed—say prayer an reckon on what parson say wid de gospel straight in 'er eye."

Let us ask Mr. P—— if he can walk the streets of Charleston without these evidences staring him in the face at every step? Custom has tolerated them, and the most flagrant licentiousness finds an apology in his arguments. Go where you will, and you find this debasing moth spreading disease in the humble artizan's domicile, and gathering around the mazes of your social castes. Virtue has become divisional, prized in one sphere and invalid in another, and men treat it as a thing of little worth—*save* what serves the needs of home. This is commented upon at home, lamented, and even censured by your better citizens.

Why deny their existence? Time and space have become annihilated by the progress of the age. Men look for themselves, and as you are not beyond the sphere of observation, they have their opinions upon the things of common observation. The proof, governed by this, places your arguments in an unenviable light, showing the weakness of your tenacity. Were it not that we know the sensitive observation of the author, we might excuse the motive, and advise him to *study life in his own city*.

We have merely traced this mingling of the species on a retrograde scale; if our learned friend wishes us to trace its mathematical details to the issue—bringing the lawful and social effects of the institution to their proper place—we will do so. The task is no difficult one, a child may point to it with unerring aim—and yet you seem not to see it.

Let us go back to the church; take these two interesting families, one setting in the richly cushioned pew, the other in the gallery. Reader, do not blush! We are only reasoning upon common principles of natural law—that is, according to the principles of Southern theology. Perhaps we should have particularized upon our own discernment, arranging the very fine traces of the combined fabric into classes, and defined the effect upon each. In this Mr. P—— must excuse us, for having wandered beyond his own depths in material metaphysics. We have no inclination to follow him, resting our apology upon the plea of indefinite latitude, and the delicate colouring it would give to his licensed Christianity.

Between these families the laws of nature have made but a small division, yet establishing the same natural affections. By the laws and customs of slavery, a parent is made to disown his own material offspring—instead of restoring them to a seat of elevation. Usage countenances the materiality in the parents, makes the mother abject, and the father ashamed of its effects. He sees the life-blood of his own being, but dare not recognize it because its spiritual life is branded with shame. Its ambition becomes ineffectual, thus hung between law and custom, and in a majority of cases deprives it of a higher transformation, making the misery that surrounds it more painful. Here the father is compelled to foster unnatural feelings to counteract natural affections—evading the natural and destroying the better qualifications of domestic goodness. This accounts for that unholy and worst phase of slavery—men selling their own children, which we have frequently witnessed, and heard denounced at the public vendue.

Thus, while Mr. P——* is struggling to establish a Christian adultery, these combined particles of Saxon and African nature are transforming themselves into a process of degeneration, hurried onward by a singular contrariety between law and custom. How is this? It is simply because these unfortunates have the same blood quickening

* Slavery in the Southern States, by a Carolinian.

through their veins that the legitimates have. They know them, with the feelings of brother and sister, but the ardour to breathe the love of brother and sister is rejected by a *point* of law, and forced obedience.

Three of this law-distrained family are females, pretty, interesting, and "likely." The pride of parentage burns within them—they speak of it, and cherish the phantom of a father's wealth; but they must only mention it to those of their class, or those who question them as friends. Here they are poised between the stimulant of pride and the force of shame. Shall they cast themselves into Afric's darkness, or proceed to transform themselves into a higher state of Saxon blood? They cannot do the latter, for the mother is the testor, and she continues to be a negro to the law, though her skin become as white as snow. She can be as black as any nigger, or as *white as any nigger*, and yet she is a nigger at last, entailing the same transcendent upon her offspring. The law rules by the mother, the father being a negative dependence. "Niggers" and white men are distinctive in the South, both in law and custom—without regard to the qualifications of the latter or the

contrasting tints of the former. This may be
right if constructed to serve a moral purpose; but
where it is made to conserve a medium of degra-
dation it becomes most intolerant.

We have seen negroes much *whiter* than whites,
morally and sightly, and yet they were held by
the thumb-screw of law, the bond property of man.
Some amusingly nice points of jurisprudence have
been developed in South Carolina, where white
men have been compelled to prove themselves
such, in order to escape the escheator of the State.
In these cases her learned Judges displayed deep
metaphysical research, and a knowledge of trans-
mutability far above their legal erudition. But
to these children.

In their own feelings they are not "*niggers*,"
and to call them such intentionally, or uninten-
tionally, would be a painful offence; nor do they
recognise their mother as such, although custom
having placed her in the category—and by law
·the property of the master, as well as his mistress,
she can be nothing else. They talk of "niggers"
just as *we* do, aspire to something more graceful,
repulsing the idea of associating with "darkies,"
and as a seeming necessity, find themselves entan-

8

gled in a mistress's guilty love—by force, consent, sales, voluntary asperities, or by a false measure of friendship.   They are all equally demoralising in their effects upon society, and may be traced to that force of law which gives one class power to hold another in an abject position, and makes necessity the mother of shame.

If the father be a good, "generous-souled Southerner," he will do well by them, and their *friends* will see them "righted."   At the same time they hang by a thread, subject to all the father's change of fortune, unforeseen incidents and impulse of feeling, and the capricious abandonment of "friends." They are still the property of his estate, and the objects of administration; and the worst features of their misfortunes is that which subjects them to the will of executors and the avarice of heirs.   We have seen this painfully carried out.   If Mr. P—— wishes us to *cite cases*, we will refer him to the judicial records of his own district.

He has given us a book setting forth the divine love of Christian adultery, over which *John Bunyan* might have wept in mimic sorrow, and *White field* shown his love for Bible texts.   As "God is love" to those who love him, so our author must have imagined his book a sunny legend of loveliness, domestic piety, and good will for those who flatter his logic while enjoying the benefit of its elements. But let us admit, for argument, that this property remains in *statu-quo ;* does not seven-tenths of it, after suffering a series of abandonment by "friends," realize its deplorable condition, and seek a lower association than the "miserable nigger ?" Our observation has brought us to this conclusion. Thus in that phase of slave-life it is working to the worst retrograde state. This is the most practical result; sometimes it is otherwise, and if they fall into strange hands and are sent off—to where, is not for the every-day business man to know—some live to eke out a miserable life of which the New Englander has no conception.

Now Mr. P——, can you stand in a city where this is but a feeble picture on the panorama that is every day moving before your eyes, and contradict your own feelings by statements that astound common sense ? Can you see specific and legalized vice stalking abroad at noon-day, filling your by-ways and market-places, enveloping it in a mantle of crime at night, and tell us it is not so ? Had you

listened to the independent voice that denounced
it, in Hibernian hall, a few months ago—pointing
out those who gave it life, and fostered its corrup-
tion—and noted the unpopular feeling that awaited
him, you would have found exceptions for Christian slavery, saving the expense of that theology
which you have founded upon the ruins of morality.

Examine its complex system where you may—
in the parlour, among the mechanics, in the field,
branches of labour about the city, or in the mistress' humble shelter, the same effects of necessity and blasted emblems of social life are there,
living in the hope of Christian adultery. We
trace the dark labyrinth where nature's mystery
hangs her veil, and there we find the cause. In
that specific construction of law—made to concert
power against a class whose lives are negative
to themselves, and while they assume to protect
them, give them no access to them—these laws
have but a statute *existence*, and are not only
made null by the social complexion of society,
but cease to be effectual through the prerogative
and popular administration of common law.
Trace the statutes of South Carolina from 1803 to

the present time, and you will find them disposing
of the rights of the slave, founded upon fear, and
made to subserve the white man's power. We
mean those which refer to the coloured population, *the acts of the assembly.* So far as the female
is concerned, her virtue is not her own, neither
socially nor lawfully. This our learned friend
will not deny, in face of the statutes and *city life
as it is.*

We can forgive him through charity, charge
his errors to that natural fault, local carelessness,
and hope that he will become a good commoner,
searching out the truths that surround his home,
and use them for the grandeur of a pre-eminent
name. Let us indulge the belief, that when he
formed the thread of his divine work he had
been studying *Bishop Butler,* and became confused in comprehending the following passage:
" It was taken for granted that Christianity was
not so much as a subject for inquiry, but was at
length discovered to be fictitious. And men
treated it as if this were an agreed point among
all people of discernment."

Such Christianity is worthy of the protection
of her chivalry, lest, like the " southern press," it

should die in the lap of her charity. It will die its own martyr ere it has truth for human ears.

We leave Mr. P——, his book, logic, and Christianity to the common sense of the common reader, and turn to W. Gilmore Simms' "Southern View."

Mr. Simms is a friend and brother, a scholar, and a gentleman of noble parts. He has done many good things for the literature of his country, and for the genius of his own State. But in keeping with the neglect of its sons, they have been slow to acknowledge it ; notwithstanding the beauty of his imagination was forced into their senses by many a "well said" notice.

In his "Southern View" of Mrs. Stowe's book, he has left the facts strewed around his own door unnoticed, and rambled through distant States for evidence against a " Yankee woman's" book, with too many truths for his own port-folio. Coming forward to lead a forlorn hope, those who smile at his ingenuity will not follow him, because they know the ground-work of his efforts. A few may share in his goodness, for it is comprehensive and kindly to their supposed interests, spreading a balmy atmosphere over their gains—but the deep-

thinker wonders at his expectations. In the
" wrath" of his surcharged brain, he has given to
the "*world*" a " Southern view," which, could the
world read it, would give him fame beyond his
"Yemassee" or " Norman Morris." He has dog-
matized the language of a lady, whose genius as
a brilliant writer, at least, should have entitled
her to common respect; depicted her motives as
infamous, obscene, and false to the core. Could we
have held his hand, and restrained him from dipping
his pen in that cess-pool of low tirade, he would
not have tarnished his purpose while struggling
to *touch* the reputation of a lady. He is the
guardian of his own reputation, and if he has set
it on a needle's point for the pleasure of the few
and faithful, it needs no foreseeing efforts to dis-
cern the consequences.

We wish it were otherwise—it is our earnest
wish, for we have admired his amiable talent,
noble nature, social qualities, and faithful motto.
Pleased with the emanations of his mind, skimming
the smoother surface of life, seldom ploughing
into the rough soil, we read them with interest.
The lack in the picture of life was made up in
the suffusion of language—and language that had

meaning. It is upon these points that he has extended his comments on Mrs. Stowe's book, endeavouring to show her an inconsistent writer; reviewing upon technicality instead of generality— upon point instead of *prima facia* construction. Let us say to those who read what we write, that when his congenial affections become quickened to a sense of the reality, his mild nature moving in its wonted sphere of contemplation, and chivalry resumes its lustre, he will look around him, and upon this "Southern View" which he has given to the world; and with pained feelings wish it back to his "Woodland home," to bury it beneath the unsold piles of his "Wigwam and Cabin."

The reading of his "*view*," its violating invective, sweeping disregard of material evidence, and struggling purpose, first called to our attention by a friend and admirer of his, prompted us to reply. In this we shall show that in his vain endeavours to smother the realities of *secret-life* in the South, he has played the unconscious fool with himself, ceased to respect his better feelings, and belied domestic wrong; that he has wandered from his home intentionally, turned his back upon the things

which belong to a *novel*-writer, for a purpose, and
struggled to drag in false policy, laid the scalpel
deeper at the root of a *good* master's interest than
Mrs. Stowe has done.   And why?

Because he has denied the truth which stands
recorded in his own district, and given the world
a ribald tirade, bearing on its face the strongest
evidence of gross inconsistency. That which denies
the whole tenor of the book with one fell. swoop,
is the strongest evidence of an ultimate intention.
The reader will detect it at a glance.   How much
better it would have been had he evinced more of
Melancthon's loving nature, acted the part of a
John Howard, going into his own city, and learn-
ing the miseries that there exist.   He would have
imparted honest intention, character, earnestness,
and an anxiety for her welfare; perhaps reduced
the number of five hundred guardsmen watching
her fears.

Our first impressions of the book were singularly different, and we cannot help referring to
them in this instance.

On its first appearance in Charleston, we were
enjoying the contemplation of Southern politics
and managerial life, their uncertainties and hope-

lessness. A little book which Mrs. Somebody
had, a few had read, and everybody denounced as
"*awful*," had *come* among us. It seemed like
Babylon disentombed for some mighty advent—a
cry of horror ascending to heaven in behalf of the
down-trodden slave. That the whole "nigger
kingdom" of the South had been killed, smothered,
torn to pieces by bloodhounds, ground up for bone
manure ; children dragged from mothers' breasts,
and whole plantations turned into slaughter-houses,
we fully expected ; and yet *nobody had read it.*
We had seen some bright pictures in the secret
life of the institution; yet we were moved with
anxiety for the book, and sent to the north for a
copy.

After a few days, a gentleman of the legal profession, whose literary discrimination upon the
true merits of a book stands second to none in
that city, brought us a copy that a friend had lent
him. "Have you read it ?" said we. "Yes."
"Then what is your opinion of it ?"

He answered us to the effect, that it was different from what he anticipated ; written with ease
and natural simplicity ; defective in style ; rather
of the Emerson school, with some of its scenes

rather highly coloured, probably for dramatic effect. "But read it, and let us have your opinion," said he.

We read it carefully, and as we continued from chapter to chapter, became more and more interested in it, for its naturalness, correct portraiture of characters, inimitable dialogue, the freshness and life of its scenes, and the display of knowledge, and grasp of comprehension peculiar to that species of Southern life, upon which the writer had founded her book. Forcibly struck with its redundant delineation, we said to ourself, "Here is a book displaying remarkable genius. Is it from the pen of a lady *novelist*, who seeks to please and dazzle the imagination? Hardly. Her power has gone beyond that, showing an earnestness in a distinct cause, at variance with a *novelist's* efforts. She has embodied the sentiments of life with a depth of research that will not fall dead on the echo—a picture of life as it is, that will go beyond a flying sketch for the parlour pleasures of the common reader. She has enlisted the intelligent and practical; and while they stand developed in reality, those who would blunder through a common sentence to quibble at her small defects,

claiming it as the beauty of their criticism, may
yet learn the power of truth from her lessons.
There is even a beauty beyond this; for in grouping
her adjuncts together, she has clothed them with
a pious sentiment, which even the sceptic must
admire.   To give divine truth its force upon the
susceptible mind, a writer cannot find a more direct
route than by contrasting the depravity of vice
with the beauties of Christian love ; to do this, it
becomes necessary to picture the coarse ruffian in
his natural garb.''

We reviewed and compared its scenes and events
—parallel ones flashed into our mind at once, and
we recurred to them one by one, as we followed
her in the thread of her narrative.   "Uncle Tom"
upon Legree's plantation seemed the worst feature.
Here Mr. Simms dwells at length, endeavouring
to establish the impossibility of such an occurrence.
In order to correct his mistake we will point him
to counterparts, in his own immediate neighbourhood.   We have seen many noble, generous, and
affectionate traits in the negro character, evincing
a hospitality and Christian forbearance worthy of
higher consideration than that we had seen mani-
fested by the chivalry.   We looked about for a

Legree, within the boundaries of South Carolina—Uncle Toms being numerous—so that we
could trace his deeds to the judicial records, where
the proof would be undeniable. There was no oc-
casion to go into " Georgia," " Virginia" or " Ten-
nessee ;" we found one of the same name close at
hand, upon *James Island, S. C.*—and from thence
we traced them in a circuit around the judicial circuit of the State. These cases are established
beyond mere topics of common conversation, and
it is to them we propose to point Mr. Simms for
the correction of his logical errors.

Again we recurred to the book, considering its
spirit and intention, and the motive of the writer.
But for the life of us, could not come to such a
conclusion as that of Mr. Simms. That it was selfish, and intended to falsify the whole South, " foment heart-burnings and unappeasable hatred between brethren of a common country, the joint-
heirs of that country's glory—to sow, in this
blooming garden of freedom," &c. &c.* * * *

We viewed it in a different light, found her re-
flections replete with good feeling for the Southerner, and pointing with unmistakable aim to au-
tocratic customs and laws, external grievances,

internal dangers, and doctrines strictly at variance
with true Republicanism.   No man can reason
upon the laws of nature, and say that deep grievances cannot exist in an institution based upon
the principle of one man being the property-holder
of another. Admitting the property-holder be high-
born, the unnatural power disposes his feelings in
the aggregate, opens a confused system of society,
spreads tyrannical vanity, strengthens the pas-
sions, and destroys the natural affections.   It
gives him the pleasure of his will, surrounds him
with circumstances that no law can govern, making
him the absolute monster of his own domicile.   In
this state of things there must naturally be gross
wrongs, and if the local powers overlook them it
becomes those who are enlisted in the good of a
common cause to point them out.   This is the intention of Mrs. Stowe's book ; and the object, aiming to correct, claims its rights—notwithstanding
Mr. Simms' dictum to the contrary.   And instead of being an "agreeable Cicerone," she has
breathed a soul of fervor into her cause, showing
an interest, deep and fervent, in humanity's good,
and entitling her to the name of a good labourer
in the field.

Mr. Simms has branded her as "a woman" with an avaricious object only. Chivalry displays its weak points in such a charge, and establishes a province of misgiving. Had it come from a low-bred man, destitute of education, an excuse might have been tolerated, but we cannot honour Mr. Simms with the same plea. That feeling and liberality which should characterise fellow-workers of the same art, had Mr. Simms shown, would have redounded to his credit, and governed him in that common respect due to the genius of a brilliant writer—much less a lady. Had he lived in an atmosphere where moral character and the genius of literature was properly appreciated, or where his own genius was respected, he would not voluntarily cast himself into a gulf of errors, reproaching when praise was deserved. His feelings would have been saved from the world's review, and himself placed in a different position to that of hand-fellow in a beaureaucratic wrong. He would have known more of Mrs. Stowe's position; compared the higher classes of society at the North with that hyper-aristocratical society of his own State—remembering the text-book of etiquette before accusing a lady in the highest *moral* walks of life, with "blasphemous" intentions.

In again recurring to the book and its appendix; "has she doffed. her modest robes and been
with us; done as we have done; sat beside the
slave-dealer—travelled with him on steamboats
and railroads—met him on the highway with his
gang chained in iron-fellowship—listened to his
self-appraised humanity rebutted by acts of *unconscious* brutality—heard him disclose, with sang-
froid shrewdness, the revolting system of his traffic, and awaiting the result, guiding his feeling
into the excitement of his history? Has she stood
with us, studying their native dialect with delight,
while they were enjoying the ecstacy of a happy
moment,—watched the dwindling fortunes of the
noble-hearted Southerner, and detesting the brute
avarice of his grasping *broker?*" She has given us
all these things with perfection, tracing the obliga-
tions of the one, and filling the fortunes of the other
with a truth that no honest Southerner can deny.
And she has ferreted out abuses—shown the intri-
cate workings of the institution, and the mockery
of laws made to govern it, with unexceptionable
correctness. Had she watched the work-house
system of Charleston, and suffered in its prison,
or gone into its poor-house, and seen the rough ends
of human nature in their worst wretchedness, she

could not have delineated them with more truthfulness.

That this species of mendacity stalks abroad unrestrained in the "queen city" of the sunny South, none will deny. And with a knowledge of them, we gave our opinion of the book then, as freely and fully as we would now, in Boston or New York. We pointed our friend to instances well known to himself, many of which had furnished subjects for better comments; the evidence was satisfactory, because it was *at home*, and could not be denied in the face of *domestic* knowledge. Here exists a great wrong on the part of Southerners, known as good masters. They tell you they know their interests are promoted by the proper treatment of their slaves, acknowledge the existence of these grievances, comment upon them, and regret the master's mendacity—and while neglecting to correct them, treasure an inveterate hatred against the voice that dare speak from abroad.

After a few days, we received a copy from the North, accompanied by a note, requesting our opinion of its merits, which we gave in a letter dated "Charleston, S. C., July 26, 1852." The following paragraphs refer to the book:

4

"I have read it with an attentive interest. 'What is your opinion of it?' you ask. Knowing my opinions on the subject of slavery, and the embodiment of those principles which I have so long supported, in favour of that peculiar institution, you may have prepared your mind for an indirect answer. This my consciousness of its truth would not allow in the present instance. The book is a truthful picture of such a life, with the dark outlines strongly portrayed; the life, characteristics, grotesque incidents—and the dialogue is life itself reduced to paper by an uncommon hand."*   *   *   *   *

"In her appendix she evades the question—whether it is founded upon actual scenes or the fiction of imagination—but says there are many counterparts, &c. &c. In this she is correct beyond a doubt. Had she changed the picture of Legree on Red river for that of Thomas L——e on James Island, South Carolina, she could not have drawn a more admirable portrait. I am led to question whether she had not some knowledge of this *   *   *   *   *, as he is known to be, and made the transposition for effect."   *   *   *

"My position, in connection with an *extreme*

party, would constitute a restraint to the full expression of my feelings against many bad effects of the institution. I have studied slavery in all its different phases—more than many have supposed, been thrown in contact with the negro in different parts of the world, and made it my aim to study his nature, as far as my limited abilities would give me light; and whatever my opinions may have been they were based upon honest conviction."

"An institution which now holds the great and most momentous question of our federal well-being, should be approached with great care. Southerners should seek out their own interests, ask themselves what they are, who are affecting them—and if bad laws do not make *bad* power? They should inquire if they were safe under such power, let right and justice govern, and act to restrain the 'bad master' who renders their defence unsafe. They see bad men coming among them, and abusing the rights which the law gives them; and they witness the disgrace of a local traffic, unblushing in its publicity, and more than foreign, because it is supported by a higher order of civilized life. And they look

upon Northerners as foes, yet never seek the best
protection against 'the enemy.' The Carolinian
seems to care little for these things; he views the
things around him as natural transcendents,
enjoys his pleasurable coldness—making force
right, military importance justice, lovingly and
thoughtfully resting the spell of his fortunes upon
the halo of glorious uncertainty. Many bless
God for their good fortune in "niggers," thank
him for making them pious Christians, and
beseech him for good returns of the staple." * * *

" He has grown up in a mental right to his own
exclusive position, looking upon everything that
is bemeaning to the slave as just and proper. He is
excusable to a certain degree, in this sense; for
that which he has been taught from his childhood
has become habitual in his nature, founding his
principles of right. With regard to the law, we
have only to watch its effects upon the object to
show the result, which is despairing in the worst
degree. At best it is difficult to carry out the intention of a law against the unyielding force of
popular sentiment; and here, in South Carolina,
there is as much consistency in carrying into effect laws made to protect the slave, as there is in

the comic-mockery of a farce-player. It is one
thing if I beat your slave, and quite another if I
beat my own. Thus we find the curse of slavery
in the unlimited power of the master, constituted
in him by the blank letter of the law, which mocks
the bondman's rights. What legislative act, based
upon the construction of self-protection for the
very men who contemplate that act, though their
policy be to show amelioration, can be enforced
when the object of legislation is held as the bond
property of the legislator? We have seen this interesting and very harmless mimicry judicially
illustrated; not so forcibly in Georgia, for there
the slave is better cared for—but in South Carolina."   *   *   *   *

"Instituting a law for the amelioration of property would seem an absurdity to many, but we
must not allow ourselves to construe it in a figura-
tive sense, dealing with the practical as it deserves,
and judging the issue. What we have witnessed
in this sense, makes us cast it to the winds, as un-
worthy the people who point you to it, as they
would to the beautiful folds of a rich flower."

"In the force of law the slave has no rights. It
distrains him as the governed, holding him in an

abject, menial, unpopular position—without caste, and without access to justice. The power of the minority fears the knowledge of the majority, and flatters with the tongue, while it seeks to crush the mental being of the slave. We speak of the institution separate from any natural law, as it is founded upon property right. Laws are strange things in South Carolina; very ancient, much honoured in the breach—seemingly made for the particular advantages of an immense school of professional *point*-makers. Every tenacious prejudice is set forth to protect a certain interest; and while justice quails under the strength of truth, an under-current is working to consolidate power against a substantive which it makes the weaker vessel. The slave works at virtuous toil, while the master grasps for power to keep him there, turning his back upon justice, and making tyranny his protector."   *   *   *   *

"Philanthropy dare not raise its voice at home, because it is unpopular, and repugnant to the *refined* ear. Nor can the voice of the governed be heard, for nine-tenths of the suffering is felt beyond the centered domain of the judiciary— allowing that the judiciary would regard them.

The negro knows this, feels his dependence, labours with strength of body against the pangs of
instinctive injustice, yet dreads to make an appeal
for fear of something more cruel.   *   *   Do
not infer from my remarks that I am seeking consolation for the abolitionists—such is not my intention.   Southerners want more workers in *black
humanity*, and more of something else to give an
honest tone to their loud and long-sounding strains
of liberty.   Cuban emancipation and *filibustering*
should begin at home, and those who *deny their
part* in the counterplot, should not *act ordnance
master to the foray*."

"In this State, he is an extra good master who
gives bacon to his slaves, measuring his ration at
a peck of corn per week.   Humanity calls for
something to correct this, and with it to enforce
his proper raiment, upon the same principle that
it is enforced in Alabama.   It is the good master's interest, and he should look to it.   Mrs.
Stowe has pointed to it directly."

"Strangers may live years in the South, pass
from town to town, in the every-day pursuits—
make casual observations, and yet see but the
'polished side' of slavery.   It has been different

with me—cast where I saw its miseries tested by
the most stringent rule of law, and witnessing the
coarse mendacity of the slave-trader and 'merchant'—the sorrows of the enslaved—its effects
upon the social and agricultural well-being of the
country, I have come to a clearly defined conclusion—it is wrong! wasting the energies of one,
and the life of the other.   With these feelings I
am constrained to do justice to Mrs. Stowe's
book, which I consider must have been written
by one thoroughly acquainted with the subject.
The character of Haley, the bankrupt master in
Kentucky, the New Orleans merchant, and the
subject of her principal scenes, are every-day
occurrences in this State, and I would almost say,
our city.   Editors may denounce it as false, and
for its *dramatic* effects as much as they please—
the tale is true! and the *occurrences* which have
taken place in this State form a picture even
more glaring."   *   *   *   *

This is from the letter we wrote at that time,
before the whirlwind of excitement was created
about this book, or Southern *poets* and *novelists*
had taken up their pens to denounce it.

Now, Mr. Simms, what does this book teach?

Is it intended as an incendiary missile, or a messenger to teach you the good of your own people?

It teaches that there are natural defects in all societies; extant grievances, wrongs, and suffering produced by the different shades of material nature; but that the moral chords may be strengthened and elevated by proper government. That when law and government make distinct classifications in the social being, giving to one distinct class power to sink another into insignificance, these grievances, according to natural laws, become greater, and deeper settled in the body politic of a State or Nation. The only question, then, is the effect—which the politician may show by comparative results. The author has pointed out the evils with a power and truthfulness that cannot be mistaken; and she has left the work for those whose province it is to trace it further.

There are defects in the book—if defects we may call them; but they are all in favour of the good master and generous Southerner. The moral diseases—the indulgences—the liberties and freedom of conversation with a good master —their tricks played with Haley, and the faithful Tom and his fortitude—old aunty in her cabin

delineator, never pictured life so natural to character as Mrs. Stowe has done.   This Mr. Simms
can find out, if he does not already know, without
going many miles from his *Woodland Cottage.*
Why has she called forth these Southern denunci-
ations and epithets?   Has she merited them, instead of the same acclamations of praise that her
countrymen have bestowed upon foreign writers
of less merit?   Are we to question her motive
and position as a lady, because she has given us
the beauty of her genius upon unpopular themes?
The calm view of the Western world will say
not!

It is because this "*Yankee Woman's*" little
book has disembodied truths that are sectionally
uncomfortable, and nowhere more so than in South
Carolina.   Her historians, poets, and *play* writers may attempt to repel them; but their attempts
will fall harmless at their feet.

Now, Mr. Simms, we will take your review:
you must go with us into the garden of your
own labours—touch not the flowers that adorn the
arbour—come within, and let us turn over, and
pull up the rank weeds that grow in the centre.
You open by saying, " Macaulay, in his opening

paragraph of his essay on the life of Addison,
discusses the question, whether lady authors should
or should not be dealt with according to strict
critical justice. The gallant reviewer gives as
his opinion, that while lady writers should not be
permitted to teach ' inaccurate history or unsound
philosophy' with impunity, it were well that cri-
tics should so far recognize the immunities of the
sex as to blunt the edge of their severity."

Had Mr. Simms so far recognized this text as
to follow its example, he would have given a national tone to his review, worthy of himself, and
free from that virulence which marks its seclusive
mania. He could very easily have gone a few
paragraphs farther, and given his readers a sentence from that learned reviewer, differently constructed, and fully establishing Mrs. Stowe's rights
upon the subject-matter of her book. The plain
reasoning of Macaulay established conclusions too
clear for Mr. Simms' liberality; and failing to
throw a shadow of misconstruction over them, he
has gratified his feelings with the following:

" But we beg to make a distinction between
lady writers and *female* writers." The italics are
Mr. Simms'. " We could not find it in our heart.

to visit the dullness or ignorance of a well-meaning lady with the vigorous discipline which it is necessary to inflict upon male dunces and blockheads. But when a writer of the softer sex manifests, in her productions, a shameless disregard of truth, and of those amenities which so peculiarly belong to her sphere of life, we hold that she has forfeited the claim to be considered a lady, and with that claim all exemption from the utmost stringency of critical punishment."

He has been pleased to class Mrs. Stowe with the "Thalestris of Billingsgate," hurling coarse speech, coarse oaths, and unwomanly blows at whomsoever she chooses to assail. This, however, is modestly, and very harmlessly, blended with a suspending clause in the next chapter. We could forgive a less experienced writer, or the aspirant seeking the congenial conquest of his own mind; but in the exercise of such language, *Mr. Simms* has openly violated the object of a reviewer, by prefacing it with the clearly conceivable purpose of his feelings. We shall not draw upon learned authorities abroad, but confine ourselves to those of South Carolina—proofs of social result, standing on the undeniable judicial records.

But we will leave this language of a French wash-erwoman, and apologize for Mr. Simms through our knowledge of the texture of excited chivalry, leaving our readers to draw their conclusions of Mrs. Stowe as an author, and W. Gilmore Simms, Esq., as a reviewer.

"She is not a Joan of Arc; she is not a fish-woman.* She is something less noble than the Gallic heroine; she is certainly a much more re-fined person than the virago of the Thames."

This is couched in a Don Cæsar-*ish* style. This is the rectified conversion of a poet's mind in a happy state.

Let us proceed. We shall come to the material points in their order, and beg the reader to fol-low us.

In speaking of her dramatic talent, and the manner in which she might have employed it to a legitimate purpose, he says:

"But she has chosen to employ her pen for pur-poses of a less worthy nature. She has volunteered officiously to intermeddle with things which concern her not—to libel and villify a people from among whom have gone forth some of the noblest men

* *Anglice,* " fish-fags."

that have adorned the race—to foment heart-
burnings and unpleasant hatred between brethren
of a common country, the joint heirs of that country's glory."

This is a common question for a common country to decide. When that fascination of state
policy, which denies humanity its rights, shall have
died away, and established principles justly acknowledged, Mr. Simms will see his error. That
the book invites itself to the attention of the general readers of his own State, is proof sufficient.
If Mrs. Stowe had incited her countrywomen to
war upon South Carolina, for some outrage committed against a foreign nation—for instance, filibustering—then the plea of intermeddling might
have had plausibility. This she has not done;
and the subject being one affecting the common
interests, national character, and general humanity
of her common country, hence her right. The
difference which Mr. Simms makes upon usage or
custom, between the petticoat citizen and the poet
citizen, are matters which we cannot enter into,
and will leave for the tenacious depths of his own
mind.

Had he viewed the book with that depth of

thought and polish of mind which he possesses in his calmer mood, he would have discovered the spirit of its intention—drawn from subjects of common conversation and observation—truths to compare with it, and saved himself from a gross charge against his own knowledge. He would have reviewed upon principle ; acknowledged that the book contained subjects for examination, affecting the political interests of the State, person and property, and moral safety, all inviting their cool consideration.

Mr. Simms again follows with a suspending clause. He says: "But whatever her designs may have been, it is very certain that she has shockingly traduced the slave-holding society of the United States, and we desire to be understood as acting entirely on the defensive, when we proceed to expose the miserable misrepresentations of her story.   *   *   *

"And in the very torrent of our wrath, (while declining to 'carry the war into Africa,') to acquire and beget a temperance which may give it smoothness."

We must answer this by first asking some questions. Did you ever, like John Howard, watch the secret character of your police—go into the miserable dens, in and around your city, where poverty and decaying wretchedness sits imploring on the door-sill? Have you darkened the iron portals of your "time-honored jail," to relieve the distressed and persecuted, or the descendants of those whose name you have emblazoned in history—inquired its regime, and asked the hungry mortals *who* starved them at the expense of the State? Scenes for your book-making are there —go and search them out—compare them with Mrs. Stowe's book, and acknowledge its truths. Have you entered that externally-beautiful, semigothic edifice, with its watch-towers and parapets, like a European castle, looming above the humble dwellings around it—and marked by the singular cognomen of Hutchinson's folly? Or have you, like many others, satisfied yourself with the dazzling skill of the artizan, worked around its spacious portals? You would have found it a *grand* municipal slave pen, with beauty without and misery within, and learned from its keeper facts pictured in Mrs. Stowe's book.

Had you turned the corner of your great banking institutions, and gone into State street, you

5

would have seen the link of money and misery. The slave-trader's fortunes are there, and the importance of his traffic held forth in unblushing boldness. His mode is no common thing, and he will point you to the samples that surround his door at noon-day, offering you fine bargains in *imps* and *aged*—tell you how shrewd he was in getting them through a mortgage—what he means to do with the mother—fat the "old feller," make him "prime No. 1," and ship him—how much "*clare*" he'll make on "that gal"—who wants t'other for a mistress, what likely proportions she's got—how the boys will make "tip-top field hands"—what titles he can give, bonds if required, and how he will arrange the separation without the least trouble. This is a great thoroughfare, and great things are transacted in it, "as well in money as niggers." Some of these establishments have pens in front, and high fences mounted with cutting glass and dangerous spikes, to challenge egress; others have brilliant fronts, with fine cushioned chairs, and walnut polished desks, to close a view of their pen in the rear. But let us pass these, and go to that rookery of sorrow at the corner of State and Chalmers' street—we

mean that of Norman Gadsden; it is more in
keeping with the misery of his trade, and if he
does deny his identity when abroad, he takes
pleasure in disclosing his strict rule of business
when at home. He will show us his pigeon-holes
for human purposes—disclose the history of his
fortunes—tell us how he made his million; and
from it you can draw a picture, in contrast with
which Mrs. Stowe's is but a shadow. There is no
trouble in doing these things, so long as you are in
the confidence.

Have you gone into the " by-ways," to learn the
sanctioned licentiousness that slavery has entailed
upon the lower classes of your society ? You would
then find intermixtures most unnatural, and custom granting it no harm; inconsistent in the
breach, and very unlawful in the abstract; granting harmony and fellowship to constituent parts
of society, and rejecting divine interposition; virtually granting a caveat to licentiousness, repu-
diating moral issue, and condemning the prerogative right of the divine will.

In conclusion, let us ask Mr. Simms if he has
not travelled on steamboats, railroads, and post-
roads, when the travelling trader was making up

his gang, enumerating his number of "*head*,"
their different qualities, the different portions of
"prime fellows," the "worked-down ones," the
work in them, the feed necessary to improve their
condition before he got to market, and witnessed
the very embodiment of Mrs. Stowe's book?

If he say not, we can only say it seems strange
that they were brought to our notice as every-day
occurrences the first season we spent in Charleston.   We should not pretend to class our power
of observation with his; and yet he tells us he has
never seen them, with as much complacency as if
he were born to overlook them.   There is something in this beyond our comprehension.   If he
has chosen to act the statesman's part, and sit in
the comforts of his "Woodland home" discussing
those all-absorbing questions of secession, suppers,
and "belly-theologies," instead of tracing out the
potent evils and secret life of his own district, tc
fill his pages with depth of character, he can hardly
claim to be excused.   His neglect has given Mrs.
Stowe a right to enter the field, and he must not
blaspheme against her labours, for they have only
disentombed the things which he should have given
us in his "*Wigwam and Cabin.*"   If he had been

up and doing the freshness of nature instead of
the obscenity of character would have decorated
his "Wigwam" and his "Golden Christmas,"
something beyond the shadow of a golden dream,
saving his invention, and doing credit to his origi-
nality.

We trust Mr. Simms will not charge us with
officiousness, when we point him to domestic counterparts of Mrs. Stowe's book, which, having
transpired near his own home, he cannot mistake
them. In doing this we shall select a few principal ones, and touch them as lightly as possible,
first noticing how negroes are brought into trouble.

The police system, based upon espionage, gives
its officers power to exert their ingenuity in the
tricks of office to extort fees; it is brought to bear
upon the poor white as well as the black, though
with more stringency upon the latter. None will
deny this, because it is carried out against party
comment. This is carried out by the power of
an elective franchise conducted upon the worst
relics of an English system, and swayed by
money-power. The secret workings and traps to
get negroes into trouble for the purpose of extorting a fee, has been carried on with shameless

disregard for many years, and it only requires a
little attention on the part of Mr. Simms to
become acquainted with its history—common conversation in Charleston will disclose it. If he
requires more particular evidence, we will point
him to G. W. Reynold's speech at Hibernian
Hall, and a writer in the " Charleston Courier,"
signing himself a "responsible citizen, September —, 1852." We will cite two or three passages from the writer's article, which display a
keen knowledge of the glaring practices. Speaking of the men who abuse slaves, and the demo-
ralizing traffic of liquor sellers, &c. &c., he says :
" At no period has its influence upon our slave
population been more palpable or more dangerous. At no period has the municipal administration been so wilfully blind to these corrupt
practices, or so lenient and forgiving when such
practices are exposed. The class to which we
refer, are unswerving supporters of God. * * *"

Considering the excitable character of society,
these exceptions of independence speak volumes.
We give them because Mr. Simms has dwelt at
length upon a particular force of law, which we
contend has little to do with justice in South

Carolina. They are themes which Mrs. Stowe
has entirely overlooked, which despoil the negro,
and bring him to a worse state of suffering than
she has depicted. The negro is corrupted by
rum-sellers, made a " bad nigger," neglecting the
commands of his master, who in turn inflicts the
severest punishment, while the law, instead of
being enforced, remains an accommodating medium for the malefactor. No dealer can sell liquor
to a negro unless he have an order from a *white*
man, without violating the law; but to continue
his avaricious purpose he makes it a matter of
dollars and cents with the police-man, who has
an ultimate object—gets pay for arresting and
punishing the negro, and reaps a double interest.
Common sense can trace this to a defective system, which is destroying the social condition of
the lower classes. Again the writer says, " We
have at this moment in our possession a certificate
from a citizen, sworn to before *Mr. Giles*, the
magistrate, declaring that he, the deponent,
heard one of the city police officers (S———)
make a demand for money upon one of these
shop-keepers, and promised that if he would pay
him five dollars at stated intervals ' *none* of the
police officers would trouble him.' "

Mrs. Stowe has only aimed *here*, in passages where she attempts to show the standard of morality.

We have seen fifty cases. For Mr. Simms' benefit, *see* Oland *vs.* State of South Carolina, who paid police officers one hundred and forty dollars in the space of six months for allowing him to violate the statutes; and because he refused to pay an exorbitant sum to *continue* was accommodated with a short residence in jail, to mock at justice. Again, we have seen an officer take two dollars from a negro to spare him from the handcuffs, while he was committing him to jail, and reported it to a judicial magistrate. We have heard a guardman, after *bell-ring*, call a negro from the limits of his master's gate, on a pretext of showing him something—arrest him, and extort a dollar from him, then pass into a *rum* shop and drink with his comrade. Could anything be more despicable? and yet the negro's testimony is black, consequently invalid, and he must be dragged to the guardhouse, and *paddled* at the work-house in the morning, unless his master appears for him and puts down the fee. This reverts to another difficulty between the slave and his master; for in nine

cases out of ten the Master will credit the statement of the guardman in preference to the slave's
explanation of circumstances.

Let us give a ridiculous instance—a wealthy,
but not very temperate gentleman, had become
jollily fuddled, and strayed from his domestic affections on a rainy night. His better half became
alarmed and despatched *Jake*, (pass in hand,) who
found his lord and master in very comfortable
quarters, about twelve o'clock at night. After
considerable persuasion, he agreed to leave the
denizens and accompany *Jake* to his happy home.
They had not gone far before it was evident *Jake*
had a task in hand, for his lord could neither
keep an upright, get his sea-legs, nor navigate the
uprising breakers of the side-walk. In a word,
he was respectably "*done gone.*" Jake had played
tricks on "Massa fo'h, an know'd 'is natur like a
book;" but he was faithful in an emergency, and
at length shouldered Massa. It rained "like guns,"
and Massa was big and heavy. After carrying
him to the corner of King and Market streets, he
was "*out-did*," and compelled to drop him on the
side-walk. Here he remained for some minutes
watching the toddied cares of his master. The

guardman in his round, found Jake attempting another tug at "*done gone Massa*," and instead of assisting to got Massa home, demanded his pass.

Jake had lost his pass, and his story, being black, was useless, even with the strength of circumstances, and he was dragged off to the lock-up. The guardman returned to the storm-stayed Master, and recognising him as a scion of wealth, took him home. And while Massa was taking long comfort in the morning, Jake was getting his paddles at the workhouse. The trounsing did not stop here, for the guardman, who *notified* in the morning, reported adverse to Jake's fidelity, stating that he was picked up some distance from home in a state of inebriation _himself. The statement was white, consequently valid and sufficient; and to punish such mischievous tricks, Massa just gave Jake a "couple a dozen" real stingers with the *family* cow-hide.

The artifices resorted to are innumerable, distorting his feelings, and violating his rights. This arises from the construction and bad administration of laws which reduce the negro to an abject condition, where he must bear the burden of all their defects. Mrs. Stowe has shown this with vivid effect, and pointed it out on a grand scale.

These are truths in full flower in Mr. Simms' own "blooming garden of freedom," untouched by himself, but cultivated by Mrs. Stowe.

As we continue we shall show that this great foundation of law, upon which Mr. Simms has built his "Southern view," is unsound; and that there is a wide difference between the statute existence of law and the administration of justice. We shall show him that a poor man's justice is a poor affair in South Carolina—that purse, power, and *point* of position have much to do in withholding the ends of justice—that those antiquated relics of England's younger days are ill-adapted to the progress of civilization, complex, uncertain, burdening justice, and oppressing the poor. That they shield unmanliness, make the *privileged* citizen a positive and the other a negative being, giving one man power to exercise his vindictive feelings upon another. This done, we shall leave the reader to judge what the position of the negro, who is held as property in the estimation of law and custom, must be; and what he has to expect from Mr. Simms' sovereign law.

In answer to his remarks on the miserable condition of the poor in Northern cities, we will refer him to a few incidents, forming parts of what came under our observation in his own city; and if he had gone with us into those miserable shelters we have spoken of, he would have found many such.

1st. A young man from the North, failing to procure work, and out of money, was driven from house to house without friends; he became sick, and would have died in the street, but for the timely sympathy of a poor negro woman, who gave him a shelter under her roof—nursed him, and shared her coarse meal with him, and when he recovered, her husband procured him a passage to his native State. He found neither hospitality nor friendship among those who make it their loudest boast. But true kindness awaited him under that humble shelter, and a friend that, as a last token, bore his trunk to the vessel upon his head, and bid him a friendly adieu, asking no other recompense than that which Heaven can give. That young man now holds a respectable position at the North, and has rewarded the kindness of his "*nigger*" friends.

2d. A poor artist, with a wife and two small children, living in a desolate room, reduced by sickness and want of employment to the worst stage of suffering necessity—his wife appealing at aristocratic doors for charity, and turned away with a cold repulse—going to a prison and begging a loaf of bread for her suffering children; and at length driven to crime. And while in this miserable condition, an officer entered with a " distress warrant;" and to make the group more pitiable, dragged off their bed and a few chairs. This is not law, but a species of tolerated injustice, practised every day by the very servitors of the law. For evidence of this, we can refer him to the generous magistrate who saved their effects from " a constable's sale in the market"—not to satisfy a rich landlord, but to eke out a fee. But it is not ended here. To crown the *point* of hospitality, when he recovered, and appealed to the commissioners of the poor—not for admittance into the poor-house, for that is considered a hospitality worthy of lengthy consideration—but for immediate relief. And after waiting nearly ten days, passing through resolves and re-resolves, he was granted a few dollars, with a provision that it be toward his passage-money to carry him beyond the limits of the State, which it was stipulated he should *leave at once.*

We have gone into his own happy State—*his* *"blooming garden of freedom"*—to point him to things that he has neglected; while saying that they could not exist there, he has pointed us to the North for objects of misery. We witnessed a worse state of wretchedness among the poor whites in Charleston, than could exist at the North—things discreditable to an opulent public, and which Mr. Simms has merited censure for over-looking.

3d. A man whose name is familiar to Mr. Simms, and who once enjoyed an affluent style of living—dying a besotted death in a filthy chamber in King street, without a friend to raise a hand for him; and two strangers taking from their meagre pockets to minister to his last suffering. Look to these things, Mr. Simms : there is more distress in your voluptuous city than you are aware of. Trace it to its cause, and institute a remedy; it should not be tolerated in a small population like yours.

4th. With reference to another question, if Mr. Simms had gone to the jail, he would have found truths occupying a large space in Mrs. Stowe's

book. He would have found that establishment
used for various purposes not consonant with the
law. He would have seen suffering and oppres-
sion in all its various shades; the petty tyranny
of magistrates, abuse of power, and violation of
justice in its worst form. He would have found
it turned into a house of peculation for the interests of a modern Shylock, who speculates upon
the hunger of human being. How is this?

The act of the Georgia legislature provides
forty-four cents a day for the maintenance of
prisoners in jail awaiting trial, &c. &c., with a
stipend regulating the food in her penitentiary.
This, so far as our observation has gone, is carried out in accordance with the act, and the jail
in Savannah being a municipal institution, is
regulated by the city authorities. In South Carolina it is different, the legislature providing only
thirty cents a day, with a stipend in regard to
the quality of bread and beef. This if for the
white man, eighteen cents being allowed for the
negro, who receives his amount in hominy. Thus
the difference between a black appetite and a
hungry white man. Even this small allowance,
were it carried out in accordance with the law,

might appease the demands of hunger; but this is not the case. Charleston being blessed with two sheriffs, the city and county sheriff, there exists an uncertain question of right to the spoils, very similar to that which her people hold upon State sovereignty and federal power. But the institution belonging to the State—and having *no* "*penitentiaries*"—is held by the county sheriff as in times of old, and he constituted lord warden over the whole. Thus it stands, a monument of peculation for those whom the law has empowered—and custom has sanctioned it as a right. An incurious public look upon those who get into such places as beyond the pale of notice; the spoils belong to the empowered, and in the absence of jail committee, *Attorney General,* or a conservative regulator, reaps his thousands from the spoliation of food. England established this system, and South Carolina continues it.

Here, Mr. Simms, are scenes for your labours; enter among them, and correct your "Southern View" of Mrs. Stowe's book.

The voice of South Carolina calls loudly against the injustice of *her* son being imprisoned in Batavia, and waiting five months for a trial;

how is it at home ? In her jails are men who, *committed without a hearing*, have lain there five, six, and seven months awaiting a trial—suffering for bread, destitute, crying hunger ; laying down upon a coarse blanket (the State's own) in the afternoon, and dreaming of food and its enjoyments, to wake to the disappointment of a dream—to know that they would receive a bit of bread only, at eight o'clock the next morning. O, proud State ! These very men are incarcerated without a hearing, and confined in the fourth story, in badly ventilated cells—suffering the sweltering influences of an unhealthy climate, and waiting five, six, seven, and eight months to be discharged by the grand jury, or get a hearing before the sessions, the city court seeming to have little jurisdiction over those who fall into the hands of the county sheriff. Circumstances of right or wrong should always claim the attention of a hospitable people for the incarcerated, and hear his cause. This is punishing the innocent according to usage, and upon the same principle that Mr. Simms would find no poetry in the negro's cause, and would not listen to the story of his wrongs, because some rich man said he was a bad nigger.

6

In that institution we will find the noble-hearted
jailer, who gets but a paltry pittance for his labour, acting the part of a father, a physician, a
penitentiary-keeper, and a jailer. You will find
him, while struggling to raise his family in the
same sphere of morality that has marked him
through life, taking the bread from his own table
to relieve the suffering of those around him. Ask
him for a history—he will point you to the scenes
which are disclosed to the letter in Mrs. Stowe's
book. He can give you his experience in punishments as a mere matter of business. Turn to the
records of the jail, and you will find fifty-four coloured seamen imprisoned in one year, on that singular charge—" *contrary to law.*" Ask who gets
the immense fees that accrue from it ; and if it is
right because of the influence without. Why put
them with " *bad* niggers" within ? The tenacity
holding these things as rights, may be reasoned
down to a *small point*.

Ask the jailer what his moral character has done
for him, in the light of contrast with those who
lord a control over him, and then establish your
philosophy of " moral sentiment."

The power of magistracy is a petty sovereignty

in Charleston. One man having a difficulty with
another, gets a warrant from a magistrate, and
without regard to the offending party, he is incarcerated without a hearing, notwithstanding the
face of the warrant contains the usual clause—
"*bring the body before me.*" There is a fee-secret
in this which Mr. Simms has never troubled his
head to solve. In this position the incarcerated
has the alternative of giving bail if he has friends,
or settling according to the stipulation of the party
incarcerating. Thus one man has power to vent
his feelings upon another, and the justice, being a
participant, settles the affair upon certain conditions, and charges the "*fees to the State.*" The
same justice will bring a " cross-warrant," and
both parties being incarcerated, they can amuse
their antagonistical feelings upon an agreed point
honourable to both, pay the justice, be friends
again, and *come out*—"*fees charged to the State.*"

We could enumerate to any extent, *citing* cases
that came under our observation. This is not
law—it is tolerated injustice, protected by a wanton
inattention. *See records;* and refer to Colonel
R. W. S——, a gentleman of high standing at
the Charleston bar—the only person who has

shouldered the Attorney G——l's business, and become interested in the removal of such grievances, and has made himself *publicly* unpopular by so doing.

5th. In the case of Hewett V——, is a valuable instance of a poor man's justice in South Carolina.   Hewett, formerly steward on board the steamship "David Brown," is committed upon the charge of defrauding "*Johnson*" to the amount of "*three ten cent pieces.*"   The object is clearly malicious, yet he is denied a hearing, and compelled to lay in jail nearly four months, without money or friends.   Finally, as a matter of compromise, he is offered the alternative of *leaving the State*, or waiting three months longer for a hearing before the Sessions.   How is he to leave it? he has no money, and the order requires two officers to guard him to the ship or steamboat, and see him safe out of sight—for which they demand a dollar each.   In this instance, the man became the drudge of the jail, at a dollar a week, and with the assistance of the good-hearted *jailer*, procured the means to pay his passage to Wilmington.   *See records.*

In another case, a gentleman is dragged from

his room at the A——n Hotel, where he had put up while passing through Charleston to his home in New Orleans. This was for a rebuke given to a person attached to the house. A meddling-justice was present at the moment, issued a warrant, and notwithstanding the gentleman's strong appeal for a hearing, or time to get bail, was marched off to jail instanter. His lady, with true womanly energy, enlisted the interposition of some *popular gentlemen*, who took up the matter, and finding he was a person of position procured his release as quietly as possible. In the presence of several persons, of which we were one, he appealed to the magistrate, inquiring if such was law and justice in South Carolina; and after several attempts to evade a direct answer, he rejoined by saying it was a right *justices* in South Carolina had. This case cannot be mistaken—and is only one among the many. Turn your pen upon it Mr. Simms—rout a tyranny that sets law and justice at defiance, before you bring up the strength of law to condemn Mrs. Stowe's book.

6th. A gentleman of the legal profession—*but* from the North, is insulted in the street by a *true* Carolinian; the guard interposes, and coming under that department the matter is brought before the Mayor. His Honour, viewing it as a small matter, very properly dismissed it, without costs. This was not the beginning of the end. The *true* Carolinian, who was the offending party, procured a warrant from a "justice," and had the other incarcerated for *assault and battery ;* and this, without granting him a hearing or giving him an opportunity to procure bail. Here he remained for weeks, among the lowest criminals, and would have remained for months, had it not been for the kindly interposition of the member of the bar to whom we have before referred, who procured his release through the Attorney-General. That young man was subject to the meanest impositions in South Carolina; but in his native city he holds a responsible appointment under the Governor of the State.

7th. A magistrate issues a "peace warrant" upon the slightest pretext. This is done upon parties who are held as having *no position*, and being poor, they must go to jail without a hearing. After a certain durance, the same magistrate will intercede for them, and on payment of an attorney's fee—for they always associate the

office with the legal profession, and work upon two
distinct angles—can procure his release. If he
has no money, he has the point of option before
him—"*leave the State*," or remain in durance vile
"a year and a day."   An instance is known where
a young man was kept in jail several successive
years and *days* by this process, merely to gratify
the feelings of a relative—and finally dispatched
his tortured existence by committing suicide in
prison.

These grievances exist in full force in your own
"blooming garden of freedom," Mr. Simms;
and we have witnessed the amount of suffering
they entail upon dependent families with pained
feelings.

Husbands put their wives in jail to please their
fancy, and wives do the same *vice versa*, all
through the medium of a magistrate, who gets
his retainer, and charges the "fees to the State."
We know an instance where a woman committed
her husband five times in a few weeks for intoxi-
cation. The State stood the fees. And notwithstanding the gallantry and chivalry of South
Carolina, ladies are imprisoned for debt—and
have to remain in durance among the sterner sex

and low criminals, weeks, months, and perhaps years—as the case may be. We know a beautiful instance which took place the present year, where a lady attempted to scale the walls, but made a singular escape *through* the modesty of the defendant's attorney, clearing the city just in time to save herself from the hands of the sheriff.

8th. Men serve their sentences, and are arrested upon a peace warrant for the same offence before they have escaped the prison doors, are re-committed, and must remain a *year and a day, or leave the State. See cases* " Miller *vs.* ——," " Comens *vs.* ——," " Kelly *vs.* ——;" the first was an inoffensive old man, who had been attached to the custom-house for a *great many* years. *Everybody* said it was a *shame*, but nobody acted to relieve him. The others were lads, and left the State in accordance with the majesty of the law.

Mr. Simms may meet us with that general re-joinder which greets those who "*interfere*" with a master when unlawfully punishing *his* negro, " It is none of *your* business." But we are among the " flowers" of his own "blooming garden," and we shall continue to the black ones, showing what they are.

This is a very profitable business for the county sheriff, and the magistrates, but hard amusement for those who are compelled to suffer in their cells, through the most dangerous season, waiting for the October term of the Court—especially when the members of the bar have power to *postpone* the setting of the Court a few weeks for their own accommodation.

9th. Here men are found nearly naked, having sold their clothes and little effects, to procure the means to sustain life : men who were committed upon suspicion of trifling offences, and had waited in jail six and seven months, without a hearing. *See* the cases of Bergen and Quail. In fact, so little attention is paid by the public to what is going on within their institutions, that a few years ago a well known *Jew* was appointed jail-master by the sheriff, and instead of respecting the duties of his office, prohibited liquor from without, and opened a *bar-room* within, selling the poisonous drug to the poor prisoners, at an exorbitant price, and taking their little jewelry and clothing, at a paltry pittance, in return. This gentleman (*Tobias*) now enjoys his wealth thus made, with as much importance as the straight-forward merchant.

We called this poor men's justice when we were in Charleston, and we call it the same now.

Now if we take into consideration that a judicial magistrate forms the highest *tribunal* by which a negro can be tried, except in capital crimes, when he is honoured with a board of three or five freeholders, we may form some estimation of the justice that awaits him. Mrs. Stowe made an error when she said: "Thank God, the slave trade has been abolished;" and Mr. Simms made a fatal one when he founded his review upon the law and the penitentiaries; he forgot that she had none of the latter.

The reader may ask us, "Why are men kept starving? you said the State allowed thirty cents a day." We answer: it is upon the same principle that laws are made to protect the slave, and remain a dead letter upon the statutes. The prisoner gets what is called a pound of bread and a pound of meat—the former tolerable, and the latter unfit for human beings. The bread costs three, and the meat five cents per pound, *as per contract*. But as no provision is made for him to cook his *meat*, he is forced to the necessity of accepting a pint of *something* called soup—reducing the cost of his allowance to six and a quarter (6¼) cents per day, leaving a profit of (13¾) thirteen and three-quarter cents per head for somebody.

The nigger gets neither bread nor meat, but is fed at a cost of about four cents a day, and he must be contented at that. Now these are gross wrongs, and could not exist in any other "blooming garden" than Charleston—Mr. Simms' *own* home. They are very unpopular themes to touch, it is true; yet a *strange* voice sounded them in the executive ear a few months ago, and, honour to the awakening spirit of Governor Means, he called for a statement, propounding fourteen questions. The question is, did he receive it as per records?

On reading a Charleston paper, a few days ago, we were much pleased to find that the *Grand Jury*, after a century of abuses, had come to the grave consideration of making a presentment of these things; but lest they should personally offend, exonerated the peculating party, and charged the blame to the sovereign State. The jailer gets none of this immense profit, nor produces the suffering which it entails. He is poor, yet *above* it; and takes from his own table to appease the craving necessities of those around him. Mr. Simms should have known these things; it was his duty, not ours. He should have searched out the *secret life* of his own city, before he told his readers that such things could not exist there, in the face of law and hospitality—pointing them to the miserable condition of the poor in New England. He should have preceded Mrs. Stowe, been a missionary among the abuses, and not fallen into those ancient *State* opinions, scouting the working system of a penitentiary, and substituting lingering idleness, aggravated necessity, and the whipping-post *in the market*, for proper correctives.

10th. We have seen a negro trader march seven negroes, hand-cuffed and chained, through the public streets of Charleston at noon-day; and yet Mr. Simms comments at length upon the inconsistency of chaining the *hero* Tom. And we have seen five white men linked in iron fellowship, on their way to the market, there to be stripped and lashed, according to the sovereign law. The affair presented an importance in keeping with the dignity of the State, and was worthy of a more descriptive pen than ours. Numerous officials, in full dress, holding long tip-staffs in

endurance. They hear of suffering and wrong—
men grasping each other's property—slaves being
dragged off—free negroes run off—slaves levied
upon—retained by stress, distress warrants, and
cruelty of bad owners—and yet they seem to
them mere every-day affairs, unpoetical and un-
worthy of their pity. The straight forward business man knows little of them, and proceeds to
the cares of his counting-room as if they were
matters entirely uninteresting to his business; the
democratic aristocrat sits smoking his cigar in the
jolly affluence of life—to accommodate his good
lady he may write an order for some " wench " to
carry to the work-house and get herself "paddled;"
the middle classes scratch for a living, measuring
the square inches of work in their employed negroes; the voice of the lower class is dependent,
and the *press dare* not touch them—just in this
proportion is the slave's wrongs left untouched.

11th. Now Mr. Simms, while the law is tram-
pled upon in your city, and the rights of the
poor disregarded, what is the power of money?
and how are favours dispensed to the man of
position? We could enlighten you with a detailed history, but will content ourselves with

referring you to one or two prominent and well
known cases : "Gatewood *vs.* State of South
Carolina ; Gatewood *vs.* Moses ; Laurens *vs.* ——.
The public cry shame; yet justice sleeps for
them, and sentences tarry by the way-side—perhaps in the Attorney-General's pocket. When
you speak of justice, remember its qualities ; and
when you name law for the slave's protection,
know that you are endeavouring to impress the
minds of your readers with an intolerant absurdity.

12th. The character of Haley, and his association with Shelby, seems to be a particular objection, and in connection with *the law*, forms particular reasons for branding Mrs. Stowe's book as
"a tissue of falsehood." Now let us go to your
own door, that you may not mistake, and point
you to pictures of perfection set forth in Mrs.
Stowe's book. Bob. Austin, Bob. Adams, and
Rumney " on Santee." The transactions of the
latter would outshine those of Haley ; while the
mendacity of the former has been more daring, and
so openly displayed in your midst as not to have
escaped your notice. You must go among them,
listen to their fine spun tests of "nigger natur,"

how they swop—" strike a trade for a gal, a
prime feller, extra prime feller, young-un; and
an old rack that a'nt got seven coppers worth a
flesh on him, that they intend to make a clare
two and two aughts upon." You must discard
etiquette, for it wont do to stand upon point of
caste, necessity waves that, but be friendly and
sociable with them, and inform yourself upon
their sacred occupation through agreeable endeavours.

13th. The reader must note the names of Bob.
Adams and Bob. Austin, for we intend to give
samples of their bold mendacity in the " sunny
city," that he may contrast it with that of Mrs.
Stowe's Haley. As for Rumney—he will give
you an exciting history of his life on the borders
of Texas—his slave traffic in the Middle and
Southern States—his connections with Bob. Austin and Mr. G——, of Charleston, and what a
cunning system he had for running off free negroes,
and " how he did'nt care seven coppers for the
law." He will tell you about his being pestered with
runaways—how he " peppered" them with shot,
" good big slugs"—let his hounds worry their
" *shins*," and finally, how he applied the stock

of his "double-barrel gun" until he made them submit with their eyes popping out. He will also tell you his revolting mode of examining wenches, before he purchased; frightening them into obedience; his punishments; trouble in separating "wenches" from their "blasted young uns," and terrors coupled with jolly times. Yes! he will give you the whole *modus operandi* of making up his gang—very cool, very unassuming, and perfectly business-like—assuring you at the same time that he is just the *"humanest* man about." That niggers have actually run to him for protection, begging him to buy them of their masters. Rumney is a right "good fellow" in his way, and you must "take somethin" whenever he asks you to join, in order to get the beauty of his knowledge. If he present his "flaming dagger," telling you what he has done with it, and how he defied the whole guard of Charleston, you must not shudder—flatter his *bravery.*

The association of his trade has made him what he is, and the good traits of his character may yet be warmed into genial nature. His history of the slave trade would make a work of immense interest. We had the *pleasure* of his acquaintance,

7

and stored our noddle with his choicest morsels.
They are of rare species—truths blooming in Mr.
Simms' "blooming garden of freedom." Rumney
will invite you to his pleasant home on Santee—
tell you how he "shoots" his neighbour's "niggers" for hunting his hogs with "*cur-dogs*" instead of hounds; and how he waylaid them in the
swamp, and nearly killed them, imitating the manner in which they jumped when he put the "plugs"
into them; and he will tell you how, when their
owners came down upon him on horseback, he
presented his "double-barrel," and bid them defiance.   He will, too, disclose a little logic in the
law, by telling you he knew they could not touch
him, for "nigger" testimony "war'nt worth a
———." *For particulars see Georgetown district.*

Here is a Haley at Mr. Simms' own door; and
marks are abundant in every district of the State,
so perfectly set forth in Mrs. Stowe's book, that
it were impossible for Mr. Simms to have overlooked them.   We therefore submit it, whether
his errors are unconscious or intentional!

14th. We must now pass to his forced doctrine,
that the slave being property, founds his master's
interest, consequently he will not abuse that which

is to his own detriment. This is straining probability for an issue—something after the principle
that every man acts for his own interest in everything. Mr. Simms should have contrasted the
subtleness of man's nature, and the power of
mental and physical action in governing his purposes, with that medium of probability which
hangs upon mere circumstance. This is a pre-
eminent point in Mrs. Stowe's book—to show
Southerners that they neglect their own interests.

Every good master will acknowledge that it is
for his interest to feed his negro well; but that
the principle is carried out, no honest Southerner
will insist. In our observation, we should class
it upon a par with asking an honest son of the
Emerald Isle, working his frame of bones in a
"gravel cart," why he did not feed that animal
better? Upon the same principle, it would be
better for his interest. Mr. Simms does not seem
to analyze the effect of circumstance. We have
witnessed many instances where negroes were
worked down by hard masters, to the last stage
of animal substance. This was done by the necessity of procuring crops with insufficient means.
In this manner gangs are sent to market in the

fall, with scarcely enough instinctive activity to support them. In this state it becomes necessary for the "broker" to put them through a process of physical "fatting," and mental quickening, before they are fit to present under the hammer.

Mr. Simms can find this out by stepping from his study into the jail, work-house, or *any* of the slave-dealer's establishments. In Alabama, the act of her Legislature provides a proper ration of meat every day for the slave, establishing a penalty if the master withholds it. In South Carolina, food and raiment is entirely optional with the master; and Mr. Simms will not attempt to deny the fact, that few masters in his State give their negroes anything but corn. We have heard the mendacity of this subject discussed with as much freedom among Southerners in Charleston, as it would be at the North. Now what is the amount of labour required of the negro? how is his physical construction estimated, and what is he required to sustain it with? We all know how far the amount of labour is graduated by the feelings of the master; but we must take the generality of plantation life, and make our estimate upon the best circumstances. Here we find that the "prime

fellow" cannot finish his task in less than nine or
ten hours, and to support his animal constitution
through this, he receives a peck of corn a week—
if "massa be fust rich rice planter," he will give
his "prime hands" two pounds of bacon with it.
Even this is a beggarly charity, when we consider
the planter's boasted affluence. This bacon is
generally rancid and oily, principally Western
sides and shoulders of "small meat," and often
very bad.

Let the reader reflect upon the natural issue of
this state of things, and he will soon see the evils
which Mrs. Stowe has pointed at with unmistakable aim.   Mr. Simms' fine, fat, saucy, shiny niggers, are principally those presented in the best
phase of city life, where it would not become the
etiquette of a *gentleman of position*, unless his
servants appeared with becoming gentility before
his guests.

The plea of property interest as a protection
is the weakest that could be advanced.

In conversation with an intelligent Charlesto-
nian, a few weeks ago, upon the system which
planters pursued in the Georgetown and upper
districts of South Carolina, where he had resided,

we asked him "why such a regime was pursued, when planters knew it was against their
interests?"

"A great many planters are advanced by their
factors beyond the extent of their proper credit,
and having exhausted their means, they are
forced to take care of their crop in a limited
period, and go upon the principle that there is
plenty fish in the brooks, and game in the swamps,
which the negroes can procure and take care of
themselves, after task," said he.

This was making no consideration for inciden-
tal liability.   "Virtually that he must steal, if he
cannot procure it in any other way," said we.

"Well, it too often amounts to that—the system is bad and to be regretted," he rejoined, with
something of a forced acknowledgment.

We will now instance a case in point, and refer
Mr. Simms to proofs.   A planter upon the Pee-
dee owned a gang of negroes, upon which a broker in Charleston held a mortgage.   There were
also several executions against the planter, and
attempts had been made to levy upon "the property;" but the mortgagee, holding valid prior-
ity, acted as his guardian; yet he was bound to

surrender them to his mortgagee as soon as his crop was gathered. His factor had advanced him upon the crop, and held a prior lien upon it. Here it would have been for the interest of the mortgagee, that the negroes were well taken care of; but, the master, although his possession was negative, his power was absolute up to a certain period, and "the property" mortgaged in a high state of the market, was at its full value according to the decline, consequently his only interest was in the amount of the crop to be gathered. He was compelled to gather his crop without proportionate means to feed his negroes, and they were sent into the market in the worst condition we ever saw human beings. Had Mr. Simms stepped to the jail, he would have witnessed the comical process of fattening and polishing the spiritual life of property. The worthy "broker," who every night thanked God that he was a good Christian, ordered the jailer to "stuff" their skins with as much meat as it "could hold," and would marshal them himself every morning—precisely as Mrs. Stowe has described. *See Condy and Poulnot.*

15th. Another point of objection with Mr. Simms, is the unnecessary brute force employed by the trader.

A single instance will show the correctness upon that point. In September last, we saw one of the dealers we have before mentioned, take a negro he had purchased to make up his gang, and after ironing him, and putting a huge pair of handcuffs upon his wrists, then, seizing them by the middle with his hands, placed his foot against the negro's heart, and uttering a fierce imprecation, made the negro brace with all his power, until the poor victim groaned under the pain. This brute force was unnecessary—the "boy" had been a peaceable, quiet creature all his life, spoke of good Master and his kindness to him with tears in his eyes. This "boy" was from Beaufort—"sold for no fault" *save* his Master's reduced fortunes. **He** was a good representative of one of Mrs. Stowe's characters.

This brute force was not to test the strength of the irons about his hands, as the dealer pretended, but to overawe the negro, and teach him what a monster he had to deal with. *See* George Ingram, jun., and Capt. Poulnot.

16th. In answer to another point of objection, we will refer to the *Boy Peter*, the property of the very Rev. Mr. Y——.

Peter, his mother, and three sisters, had been the pious, favoured, and respectable servants of this Rev. gentleman from childhood. With him reverend nature was just like many other good men's—not impregnable to frailty. The changes of fortune fell upon him, and he struggled under Mr. Simms' particular necessity "*i. o. u.*" Peter was jail'd for the market, with a pledge of honour from his Master that *he would* not sell him out of the city, or away from the family, and that he would give instructions to Mr. McB——, his " broker," to that effect. Affairs became pressing, money short, nigger not sold, price did'nt suit, conditions wouldn't stand—and the "broker" played his man upon the point. Finally, the Rev. gentleman, in order to save his scruples, sold Peter to the "broker." Here he went through the usual routine of tests before customers, such as quick-step "monkey-shines," knockings on the chest with the full force of the "broker's" *fist*, standing against the wall, and having his lower jaw and his "shins" rapped with a whip stock to show how he could jump, and all without effecting a sale. This may seem strange to the distant reader, after all such means had been taken to display his merits of sale, and particularly his good disposition—which means humbleness. But they are only little flowering truths bespotting the paths of Mr. Simms' "blooming garden of freedom."

It is soon settled that the "*boy*" must be shipped to New Orleans, but Peter will not believe it, for "he no *Buckra* unsartin, but Massa too big Christian to betray confidence so." It was too true for his feelings, and in a few days he found himself manacled and marched off to join the chain-gang. We, with several others, witnessed this scene, and our object is to place it where you cannot mistake the object.

The poor fellow begged with tears in his eyes for time to see his " Old Massa," and his mother and sisters once more. Was he allowed it?—No! he was kicked out of the door with his manacles on, and the jailer ordered to put his old mother, who visited him while he was "caged for market," up in the cells to satisfy another claim. *See Records.*

No writer ever portrayed scenes, nor delineated character with so much perfection, as Mrs. Stowe has done the associations of Haley and Shelby.

17th. Eliza! It seems impossible, to Mr.

Simms that the heroic nobleness of such a crea-
tion should exist under a dark skin—no matter
what her extraction may be. In order to be as
comprehensible as possible we will point to the
Eliza, a piece of property once owned by the
same very Rev. gentleman, who failed to make
her his mistress, through her firm defiance—and
caused a domestic eruption in his household. We
must not venture beyond a point of delicacy;
yet she was an Eliza with daring virtues. Sit
down by her and hear her story, Mr. Simms—
the public know it well. The cause of her being
sent off—her miserable condition when in the
slave-dealer's hands—her mother's appeal, and
the manner she was found and brought back by
a gentleman in your city, would make a narrative more glaring than the picture of Mrs. Stowe's
Eliza. We could point to a dozen such Elizas
in your own city !—how strange that they should
have escaped your notice. The fact may be,
simply, a small difference in the measure of mind
between Northerners and Southerners, one viewing them as "horrible" outrages upon human
nature, the other, as things common to ordinary
life.

18th. For specimens of St. Clair's establishment and change of fortune, we cannot do
better than to refer you to George street. Ask
who lives in those old noble looking Doric edifices,
and listen to the oft repeated answer—there is a
legend in it! They tell you—"O, bless me, yes!
it was once the mansion of the *so-and-so's*—one
of the '*first families*,' but they are poor now—*it
was a sudden downfall*. Mr. What-you-may-call-
um owns it now; they say he did'nt get it honestly.
There was a long *suit* about it, and poor so-and-
so died miserably poor at last."

You will find the portrait of life there, and in
many other streets of Charleston. Those noble
old *castles* have changed with the circumstances
of their owners, from time to time, and the transformation meets the observer's eye at every
glance, and has been developed in detail by Mrs.
Stowe, who holds its secret history at the point
of her pen.

19th. We now come to the great point upon
which Mr. Simms has joined issue with Mrs.
Stowe;—the existence of a Legree, his cruelty
to uncle Tom, and what would be the result if
such a thing should occur.

By the laws of South Carolina, it is a penal
offence to "*run off*," or sell freemen into slavery;
yet no person in Charleston, acquainted with the
workings of slave-dealers, will question the fact
of their being "*run off*," or of its being of frequent
occurrence.   Now let us ask Mr. Simms to point
us to an instance where the penalty was enforced?
Again, he will not deny that masters have brutally
murdered their slaves.   Have they suffered the
penalty?

We will now *cite* Legrees and "Uncle Toms,"
and if Mr. Simms requires the particular history,
revolting as it is, we will give it in detail.   On
"James' Island," *near at hand*, is the gentleman
we have referred to before.   Mr. Simms cannot
miss him, and the neighbours will disclose the history of his tyranny.   Many of his punishments
were similar to that of his namesake on Red River,
with the grave exception of his tying them to trees,
and leaving them, cut and bleeding, all night.   If
this is not sufficient, we will go to the plantation
of a certain Mr. Butler, at Beaufort district, where
transactions well known to the public at large
have stained the name of civilization.

To be more unmistakable in our citations, we

will found them upon records of Court—here we
l eg Mr. Simms to follow us into Edgefield district.
Here the case of *Harden* vs. *State of South Carolina*, presents one of the " best boys" in the State
murdered in the most brutal manner; and the
cause—the lust of the master.   The evidence is
that Harden, assisted by his overseer, took the
"boy" to a corn-shed or barn, stripped him, tied
him to a rack, and lashed him with a cow-hide in the
morning and afternoon, until the flesh became hag-
gled upon his back.   Not satisfied with this barbarous ferocity, he went to the bloody spot on the
following day, and again, with the assistance of his
overseer, drew the victim's head and feet together
with ropes, and committed a barbarous outrage
upon his body, which not quite ending his life, he
dispatched it with a wooden weapon a few hours
after.

What was done with Harden?   Will Mr.
Simms tell his readers, or shall we ?————He
fled the State, and his overseer cleared himself
by turning State's evidence. As soon as the little
excitement was over, the *black death of a black
" nigger"* subsided.   Mr. Harden returned, gave
himself up to the power of accommodating justice,

was tried at the fall term of the Court of Sessions—and notwithstanding the influence of a *report* that the deceased had attempted to commit an outrage upon a white female—the case was too revolting, and the evidence too positive, to admit a doubt upon which the jury could clear him, and he was found guilty of wilful murder.

"Was he hung?" the reader will ask. Hung indeed!—hang a *white* man for killing a "nigger!" ah! that would be a pretty principle to establish against the sovereignty of the institution. No efforts, save those of constrained necessity were made for the rigour of the law, while the *great* talent of the State was arrayed for the defendant. He appealed to the "Appeal Court," the appeal was granted, his bail continued, and that tribunal ordered the case back for a new trial. In the course of a year, the case was again brought before the Court of Sessions, where the jury, after mature deliberation, brought in a verdict of manslaughter, with a suspending clause recommending him to certain mercies. Is he to be found in one of Mr. Simms' "penitentiaries?" No, reader, he was allowed to do as all gentlemen do, and was simply pardoned by the executive in consideration of the verdict. Forgetting the absence of penitentiaries in South Carolina was an oversight in Mr. Simms.

Follow me into Darlington district, and examine the case of *Benton* vs. *State of South Carolina*. Here *a man* died one of the most brutal deaths that the force of mind could picture. He is dragged to a blacksmith's shop, his tongue seared and almost drawn from his head with red-hot tongs —then stripped, and branded upon indecent parts of his body, and the next day again tied up and lashed, and left in a miserable place, where he died in less than twenty-four hours—a more torturous death than that of Mrs. Stowe's hero. These things may startle the more sensitive feelings of mankind; and we hear voices around us saying, "you do wrong to tell them abroad"—but they are truths which should be ferreted out and exposed, and the perpetrators of them made to suffer that condign punishment which they deserve, for through them the good master suffers.

Where is the offender in this case? Accommodating justice granted him bail, and he is a gentleman at large, after making a short visit into North Carolina. *See Dr. Boise and Mr. Prince* of Darlington District.

Now let us point to a more recent case, and await the issue of justice there. The case of *Craig*, charged with the murder of his slave. This case was to have been tried a few weeks ago, before the Court of Sessions at Laurensville, Judge Evens presiding. There is a revolting history connected with this case; and yet we know the complexion of society so well, that we can anticipate an *honourable* acquittal, or a peremptory pardon, if found guilty.

Can the reader imagine how these things have escaped Mr. Simms' observation, that he should have made no allowance for them in his "Southern View?"

20th. Upon another particular point of objection, which is brought up in the shape of a general *pot-pourri* of characters and property interests, we will refer to the well known case of *Bella Martin*.

This case is attended with threefold more mendacity than anything in Mrs. Stowe's book—the principal feature making it so, being that of the *State* trying to reduce human beings from a state of freedom into that of slavery. There is history and misery enough in this case to fill a volume, and yet it lies buried among the things of local life.

8

Bella, " a likely wench," lives in a little cabin at Walterboro, in the State of South Carolina, labouring at honest toil.   According to *usage*, she becomes the wife of a mulatto man, and the issue is " a likely daughter."   In the course of years, this daughter becomes the mistress of a certain Mr. Price, and the issue is three children—Benj. Price, Anna Price, and Eliza Price—the former becomes a " tip-top likely fellow," and the " gals " are extra fair to look upon.   Hence, Bella is a grandmother.   But, in the meantime, " Martin " (a widower with three sons) steps in, separates Bella from her mulatto lord, and takes her unto himself—*hence* the name of Bella Martin.   Price, the father of the three children, " *dies out*," and the mother dies a premature death.   At this juncture Bella and her grand-children are the property of Mr. ——, who threatens to sell them " off," unless Martin—who was a man of " property "—becomes a purchaser.   Martin assented, paid the purchase money, and received his bill of sale according to the conditions.   Hence they were his for any purpose.   Martin has children by Bella, but they all die at an early age.   His sons by lawful wedlock become desperate charac-

ters, and attempt to squander his property in
riotous living.   He is compelled to distrain them,
and finally abandon them to their dissolute fate.
They make an attempt to get his property upon
the plea of their father's insanity, before a court
of justice.   Failing in this, they attempted to
"*run off*" the children, but only succeeded in
carrying off, beyond the limits of the State, one
small child.

Martin died a friendless death; but anticipat-
ing the fate of Bella and her grand-children, be-
queathed them their freedom, which was set forth
in his will, and also by papers which he *thought*
to be in accordance with the law.

"Jones" is the executor of Martin's "property," and during his life saw it righted—but he
died, and his son-in-law, *Hudson*, succeeded him.
And being an avaricious man, he began to make
advances to get possession of the " property " for
his own benefit and behoof. Bella, becoming aware
of this, moved to Charleston neck, where she lived
in want and misery several years. Martin's sons
have also moved to Charleston, where one died a
besotted inebriate, and the others have become miserable specimens of loathing nature. Another

plot is propounded between them and Hudson to
dispose of the three children, and by flattering
Bella, they induce her to become a third party—
necessary to its success. This fails, and finally,
one by one, the two sons and Bella died wretched
inebriates, in a miserable hovel on " the neck."

The three children are now alone, acknowledged
as free children ; the girls work at dress-making,
and the boy is with a Mr. Johnson, who, with Mr.
Hoppo, act as the reputed guardians of the three.
And here quiet prevails for a time.

Incited by the love of gain, Hudson makes his
last grand attempt to put the value of the "property" in his pocket. He enters into a fiendish
plot with the aforesaid Bob Austin and Mr. Gilchrist, a " broker." A bill of sale purporting to
be from Bella Martin to Hudson, with the value
of the three children, price paid, &c. &c., lays
the corner stone. With this Gilchrist is to proceed, carriages and other means are at hand, and
Bob Austin is to run them into a distant State.
When there he is to put them into the hands of
another "broker," the correspondent of Gilchrist,
who, with the specific understanding that exists
among them, will sign the bond necessary for

their sale—and they are slaves for life. While
these papers were being arranged, a little yellow
boy overheard the plot, and warned the children
a few hours in advance of the officers. They in
turn, living on the alert of chance, knew the
work-house keeper, Poulnot, for his kindness to
them on former occasions, and fled to him for protection. He shut the doors of the prison upon them
as he would upon some harmless animal seeking
its escape from the savage ferocity of wild beasts.

Here they remained fast, under the lock of the
keeper of the prison; and entered upon the cal-
endar, by consent, as committed by Messrs. Hoppo
and Johnson, "guardians." This was necessary,
for they had no right to commit themselves, and
the keeper would be liable for the consequences
unless sustained by responsible names.

Gilchrist, with Bob Austin and a posse, at noon-
day repaired to the residence of the "*property*"—
but it was gone. They followed it to the work-
house, and producing the aforesaid bill of sale,
demanded the "property" from the custody of the
keeper, threatening him with imprisonment if he
refused. *Poulnot*, honour to his name, for it will
stand as a lasting record of firmness in behalf of

humanity, refused to give them up, daring them to attempt a rescue! He is persecuted, a suit is instituted by the Hudson party, and another demand is made, with papers and *satisfactory* certificates, but he holds on as firm as ever, refusing to give them up until the case is decided by the Court. *Northrop* appears as attorney for the *wreckers*, and after a shameful display of legal rascality, demands them, papers in hand, for the *pirates*.

The possession of the "property" is now turned into a piratical chase, upon which several enjoin their *honest energies*. In addition to Northrop, *Tupper* appears as attorney for a Mrs. Price, who claims them by a singular technicality of relationship with the father. And finally, to cap the climax, *Ford*, the escheator of the State, interposes his claim on behalf of the State, demanding that these poor victims be sold on behalf of his sovereign client. Here they are in prison, awaiting the sitting of that court which is to decide a question, which to them is liberty or death.

After a long history of dark villany, which we cannot recount here, Anna died in *child-birth*, alone, and within the narrow confines of a dark cell, presenting the appearance of a ghastly corpse

to the turnkey who opened the cell in the morning.
At this juncture, the "generous hearted" Magrath,
a gentleman who has honoured his city, if his city
has never honoured him in proportion, came forward as their attorney, and the case was brought
before the Court of Sessions in Charleston, October Term, 1844, Judge Withers presiding. The
evidence elicited, the mendacity of the slave-dealers, the statement of the prison-keeper, the appearance of the children before the Court, and the elo-
quent and feeling appeal of Magrath in behalf of
their freedom, would form a subject fraught with
more miseries than Mrs. Stowe's book has set forth.

This case excited some interest at the time,
and called forth a redundance of legal quibbling
that would have disgraced the name of honor in a
pirate's profession.   Will Mr. Simms tell us what
was the issue of this long and tedious case ?

The characters of Austin and Gilchrist were
exposed—their testimony impeached, and the bill
of sale purporting to be from Bella Martin to
Hudson, *and in the handwriting of Austin,* by a
singular incident shown to be a forgery. It was
further shown that Hudson had attempted to sell
them before, and that Mrs. Price's claim was

invalid, she not being akin to the father of the children; and yet Martin's will, which must have transcended to Hudson, cannot be found.

The jury, after mature deliberation, render their *conclusion* that, although the children have produced no proof to assert their freedom, they are not the "property" of the claimants, *Hudson* and *Price*—remanding them back to the custody of the prison keeper and their guardians. Thus the question of life and liberty was now between them and the sovereign State; and it remained for Mr. Ford to bring his suit upon another ground, in order to throw the amount of testimony upon the children.

Poulnot was on the alert, and having no order from court, delivered the "property" to its guardians before the escheator had time to levy.

The boy was disguised, and ushered out of the State as quick as possible, and now lives a respectable citizen in a northern city. The girl had become connected with a young German, who was as much attached to her as if she was his lawful wife, and would not consent to her leaving the State, but kept her locked up in his house, promising to defend her at the issue of life and death.

But the mendacity of the negro traders did not

end here ; soon after the decision of the jury, and
in the face of the court, an attempt was made to
wrest them from the custody of the officers, and run
them off. This being frustrated by a summary
process, we must trace the victim, Eliza Price, to
her friend's (Ashe) house, where she remains under
his lock and protection for nearly three years, and
dare not go into the street, lest she should fall into
the hands of the officers whom the escheator had
placed to arrest her. How is this? the reader
will ask, and the Carolinian will tell you how necessary it is for the benefit of the slave.

It is by one of those strange acts made to despoil the power of a majority, and crushing a few
"free coloured" while aiming to protect the white
population. By the act of the legislature of 1821,
the power of emanumition, which formerly existed
in a board of judicial magistrates, is reverted to
a committee of the House, and so burdened with
provisions as to render it almost impossible for a
majority of masters to manumit their slaves, if
they felt disposed, unless they sent them immediately out of the State. The principle features of
the provisions being the deposit of a heavy collat-
eral fund, and enormous bonds for the good beha-

4

viour of the "property"—that it will not become
a town charge, &c., &c.   In default of this the
State renders the "property" subject to *escheate*,
and the slave is sold on its behalf without any re-
serve for *its* condition in the hands of subsequent
owners.

These children were born slaves by inheritance
of the mother, and had not proved their freedom,
nor had Martin, by his will, conformed to the re-
quirements of the statutes.   Hence it becomes the
escheator to get his fees, and look after the State's
interest—and thus the action.   Three years she
remains in durance under the protection of Mr.
Ashe, when, on the 22d day of October last, during his absence from home, under an impression
that the matter had ended, the officers broke into
his house, dragged Eliza and her young child off
captives of the law, and committed them to the
custody of the work-house keeper, there to await
an order of sale from the Court.   She cannot
prove her freedom, for she is deprived of the
means; so we shall await the issue between this
poor, last remnant of fortune's misfortunes and the
State's pride.

Had Mr. Simms lent a listening ear to the long

train of miseries connected with this case, and
sifted the evidence with the feelings of one enlisted in the cause of humanity, he would have
saved a Southern reputation as well as a "Southern
View." You have said to the world that the book
was a tissue of falsehood. We say to the world,
these are the truths of Mrs. Stowe's book, staring
you in the face; and before you again raise a pen
against them, go to that municipal slave pen, "the
work-house," with its four hundred pens, to measure the square inches of human length and
breadth; and in one of these cold cloisters, on
the second floor, you will find Eliza Price and her
child. Her cell is seven-by-four feet, or nearly,
and if you cannot get *into it*, call her to the door—
sit down by her, ask why she was put in there
instead of the jail? study the point of law it was
intended to evade, and listen to the story of her
wretched life. Imagine it just as full of poetry
as if it came from white lips, for her soul is *white*,
and her lips are nearly so; then give her that assistance which it behooves a good Samaritan, or she
will be sold into slavery for the benefit of the State.

21st. While Mr. Simms is at the work-house,
we cannot better answer another point of his

titled to a hearing before a proper tribunal; but
they had no money, consequently unable to procure counsel to proceed for them.   They offered
to work if an attorney would take up their cause,
and we used our endeavours to procure one for
them, knowing they were unsafe in their position,
but justice had no life for them; and their cause
was so *unpopular* that we could enlist nobody.

The official by-play connected with slave-dealers
and magistrates would be a good subject for Mr.
Simms to study.   It would not only enlighten
him upon the theory of moral honesty, but
strengthen his views upon home subjects.   But
they were got away by Bob Adams, and how did
he effect it ?   Why he proceeded immediately on
to Mississippi with his gang, leaving the affair of
the McKims' in the hands of his " broker," Mr.
O—— ; here he procures the services of a dealer
in the *art*, with whom he is interested, and very
soon an affidavit is returned to Charleston, charg-
ing that they " are runaways" from a *gentleman*
in that State.   Mr. O—— produces this affidavit
before " Gyles," the matter of dollars and cents
is arranged, and he issues his order of discharge
to the jailer, and the slave-dealer is in possession

of his "stolen property" again. The "broker," Mr. O——, manacled these men in our presence. "Where are you going to take us?" said Caleb, as the chains were being put upon him. "To give you fifty a-piece, and then hang you, you ——!" said the broker; and they were taken to the work-house, where they were confined to evade another *point.*

Now, Mr. Simms, trace these boys into Hyde County, North Carolina, and you will find they were free. Caleb sailed Franklin Benden's boat to Newburn for several years, and Alexander run F. Jones' flat from Beaufort to Newburn. This is but one case among the many home truths growing in your own "blooming garden of free-dom." You cannot point to an instance where the penalty for running off free negroes has been carried out.

The whole lawful strength of Mr. Simms' "Southern View," for the condemnation of Mrs. Stowe's book, rests upon the following citation, which he gives us after several columns upon its general merits. Speaking of the killing of runa-ways, and the clearness and precision of a "South Carolina judge" upon the subject, he says: "We cannot forbear quoting his dictum as directly in point. In the case of Vetsell and Earnest and Parker, Colcock, J., delivered the opinion of the court," as follows:

"By the statute of 1740, any white man may apprehend and moderately correct, any slave who may be found out of the plantation at which he is employed. And if the slave assault the white person, he may be killed; but a slave who is merely flying away cannot be killed. Nor can the defendants be justified by common law, *if* we consider the negro as a person; for they were not clothed with the authority of the law to apprehend him as a felon, and without such authority he could not be killed. January term, 1818, 1st Nott & McCord's, S. C. Reports, 182."

We coincide with Mr. Simms in reference to the clearness of the "learned judge's dictum:" it is so perfectly clear the legal gentlemen, slave-hunters, and cruel masters may drive their points "right" through it, founding their legal discrimination upon its *if!*

22d. The offering a reward for the apprehension of runaways, *dead* or alive, is another strong evidence against the book in question. We admit

that the singularity of this part of the book would
seem strange to the distant reader's mind; but it
must be remembered that castes and societies are
differently organized in the South from those in
the North—more distinct, and at greater variance
with each other.   Among the lower of them, there
exists a species of desperate recklessness, priding
itself in disregard of common rights.   South Carolina is blessed with a large portion of this semi-
barbaric species, who form a melo-comic contrast
to that polished refinement so much boasted of.
They are called crackers, pin-*e*-woods-men, sand-
pit-*ers*, wire-grass-men, &c., &c.   They are a sort
of squatter ("landholders"), with little or no education—owing to a wretched system of schools
in that State—and live principally in log huts on
the barren tracts of land.   At certain seasons of
the year they scruple at no occupation, however
menial, and have a slang cant peculiar to themselves.   They always have a little patch of corn
growing, and always have a stock on hand; and in
their efforts to keep it good they frequently feel
the planters' shot about their heels.   There is an
Indian primitiveness about them without any of
the Indian's nobleness; their highest ambition is

roaming the woods with rifles and double-barrel
shot guns, hunting the planters' hogs, runaway
niggers, or killing a deer.

Mrs. Stowe's Kentucky bar-room is a perfect
picture of a " Tavern" at the crossing filled with
these men, when the *candidate for Assembly* gives
his *"free-will"* feast.

They are sure marksmen, and in hunting negroes would think no more of killing one than they
would a dog; we can point Mr. Simms to a dozen
cases.   The planters stand in fear of them, and to
punish their depredations is sure to be returned
with firing the woods and demolishing fences.
Two particular cases are of recent occurrence.
One of them, Vaigneur, took deliberate aim with
his double-barrel gun, and shot a lady dead while
standing in her own door.   This was done with
public coolness, in the town of Gillisonville.   We
visited him in prison, and he unfolded to us a history which, perhaps, few in South Carolina know.

Another became so "entranced" with the appearance of a young lady's watch and chain, (a
school teacher,) that he "brought her down" with
his *double-barrel* gun, at the door of her school;
then tearing the jewelry from her lifeless body,

9

put it about his neck, and deliberately walked into
the town. In a state of society like this, and where
so many fatal rencontres are taking place among
better citizens, our knowledge of the inconsistency
of things leaves us no compunction in believing
that negroes are killed by such men ; in fact, we
know they are. We might instance the case of
Jones and Pridgeon, in 1850. One negro was
killed, and the other drowned himself in the Savannah river ; and we know that singular rewards
are offered for their apprehension.

On asking a gentleman why he offered a reward
of seventy-five dollars for the apprehension of a negro sixty-five years of age, who had been absent two
years, " To kill the d—d old rascal," he replied.

We have a letter in our possession from a highly
respectable and good master, sent to Pridgeon,
a negro catcher, offering a hundred dollars for the
recovery of his (bad) negro fellow, who had been absent more than a year, adding that he did not
care so much for the worth of him, but was determined to have satisfaction out of him ; " and if you
can't catch him any other way, shoot the ——"

We must have stronger proof than Mr. Simms
has given us before we can condemn the book, even
here.

23d. We come to that point which Mr. Simms, following the voice of several others, has denounced. The reader must not judge from the rules of law laid down in the State cited by Mr. Simms, though we are free to admit that mothers are more frequently *sold from* their children than children from their mothers. Means of evading the law are always at hand, and the force of necessity supercedes—even in "Virginia," where a striking instance came under our observation on the 30th of November last. It is well known that common law takes precedent over those made to invest the negro with rights; we will instance a case in Charleston. B—— owned a "wench" and her child about three years and six months old. B—— is indebted to C——, who holds a mortgage on the "wench;" he is also indebted to Mr. R——, a grocer, who seizes the child and sells it in satisfaction of the debt—and is sustained by law.

We have seen a child levied upon, and sent to jail to satisfy the demand of one creditor, who receiving his claim from the owner, she was held under a detainer for another, and finally sold, the owner not being able to raise means to discharge the second debt. It was fatal for Mr. Simms to wander beyond his own State for validity, when

he knew none existed. It shows a direct intention, and want of moral courage, sufficient to give
us light from home.

24th. We now come to George Harris, and upon
such a noble character in the person of a negro,
Mr. Simms takes particular exceptions. He wants
a character; and we could not present one in
more perfection than the boy "Nicholas," who
caused the emeute in 1849. A hero of nature, but
not of the world, for an allwise Providence had
clothed him in a black skin.

There are far more exciting incidents about
Nicholas' character than that of George Harris'.
Nicholas was a stucco-worker—one of the first in
the city. His master, Kelley, a known tyrant,
promises him his freedom on payment of a stipulated sum. The boy labours at extra work until
midnight every night, burning with the love of
freedom within him. After paying more than a
third of the sum, he was defrauded by his Master,
and when he sought for justice, denied it! With
the natural feelings of a man basely defrauded
out of that which he earned by the sweat of his
brow to purchase freedom, he became incensed
against his Master, refused to pay him his hard

earnings any further, and bid him defiance! He is tortured, sent to New Orleans, brought back again, and yet refuses to give his oppressor the sweat of his brow. He is placed in the slave-pen of Norman Gadsden; here he suffers again, declaring his intention to die in the struggle for his rights. An attempt is again made to send him to New Orleans—he disarms the slave-traders, and swears he will not be separated from his family associations. McNamara, and other constables are brought to seize him; but he has become like an enraged demon, and they are forced to capture him in his pen, as they would a brute. He has left the scar of his weapon upon McNamara, and notwithstanding he is thrown into a cart, and taken almost lifeless to the jail, he has injured the majesty of the law. Here cruel tortures are resorted to, with a view of extorting a confession from him, which is at length done. Animal life and mental soul is subdued at last. He is tried before a court of *three freeholders*, and two judicial magistrates, found guilty, and sentenced to be hung. A kind voice is raised for him, his case carried to the appeal court, and a new trial ordered, on the ground that evidence had been extorted by cruelty.

Again he is tried, found guilty, and sentenced to three years' solitary confinement, with five paddles each month. The keeper of the prison finds his genius worth a treasure, and instead of regarding the sentence, sets him to work at ornamental stucco, and makes a profit by it. The law has separated him from family associations, and he falls in love with a young mulatto woman, who is for sale by Gilchrist and Bob Austin. They go to remove her from the prison, when his soul and body again becomes fired, and he swears he will die before they shall take her from the yard, driving-slave dealers, keepers, and everything else before him. The mayor is sent for, but during the interval Nicholas calls on his fellow-slaves to join him. They seize weapons and follow his lead; and as the mayor, with his posse, opens the gate, his arm is broken, and he laid prostrate on the ground at Nicholas' feet. Here is a George Harris at your own door—one which soars far above that of Mrs. Stowe's book. Trace it to the wrongs of a cruel Master, and the mendacity of slave-dealers, and you have the disease working into the very core of your social well being.

25th. As Mr. Simms has commented at some

length upon her fault as a dramatist, we must give
it a passing notice.   It is somewhat remarkable
that men seldom know their own faults, and in the
remarks upon her dramatic defects, and the singularity of position between George Harris and
Uncle Tom, we have strong evidences of it.   Mr.
Simms should have been the last writer calling
this subject into question.   He must remember,
that so far as the stage is concerned, rules of criticism have materially changed, as well as the
point of pleasing different audiences.   The rule of
inevitable catastrophes in every scene, for effect,
is known to have been repudiated by good cri-
tics upon playing, for while it aided to continue
an excitement in the feelings, it confused and
impaired the general plot.

But let us turn to the material merit.   The object of the author is clearly defined, showing two
principal phases in the slave's life, that of the old
man passing through the usual course of incidents
in such a life; the other, in a higher sphere, among
that large class of mixed Saxon, whose high blood
cannot endure the wrongs of his Master's lash—
determined upon liberty, and braving the perils of
attaining it.   Now, according to Mr. Simms, she

should have brought them into one atmosphere! Could she have done this against an absurdity which presents itself at once? The roads grading into the depths of slavery are on the one side, and freedom on the other. How then could she have combined the threads of her narrative upon one detailed path, and given the strength of reality, extent of research, and embodiment of the general subject with the grasp that she has? To us, considering the subject of the book, it is a beauty of foreseen plan worthy of admiration instead of condemnation. What struck our attention most forcibly, was the strength of ingenuity displayed in grouping the tableaux of her last scenes. Here the dramatist finds a picture for a beautiful finale, without transplanting it with different language and adaptation. Put a book into the hands of a manager to be dramatised, and brought out upon the stage, he views the arrangement of characters— the quality of language regulated according to the position of the *dramatis personæ*, the general merits of the subject with regard to effect upon country or community, and the point of interest at his own door. We may differ from Mr. Simms, though he is aware that we have examined his books for dramatic purposes, but we cannot see how a person with true dramatic knowledge can read the book without seeing the adjuncts of a fresh, life-like piece for the stage before him. Each character is adapted to the business of actors according to their different ranges, and with language in their mouths embodying their own character. Can we turn to Mr. Simms, and say the same? If Mrs. Stowe were at fault she could find no better excuse than to curtain herself behind the dramatic defects of Mr. Simms; perhaps we should have made an exception, for Mr. Simms has never reached a dramatic scale. The "Wigwam and Cabin," unnatural with its scenes thrown in juxtaposition—characters loathing with obscenity, in their shadowed life, and language of insipid vulgarity in their mouths, to give them an epic nauseau without unfolding the embodiment of life, are there. We look for a plot to give it life—we look for the points that we may localise it, and bring it upon the stage, but they are not there, and we are forced to abandon it.

Let us turn to the "Golden Christmas;" a pretty story drawn from amiable genius, to show the sunny side of pictured life:—let us search

among the Ned Bunner's, Paulla Beanseux' and
Beatrice Mayzek's. We find a shadow of the
mere object, devoid of language to give character
and effect. Nothing from which we can draw the
material of a piece, unless we tear down the whole
structure, and rebuild at a greater expense than it
would cost for an original. We may look them
through—but the beauty of character with which
Mrs. Stowe has embodied St. Clare, and the soul-
stirring love of that sweet child, who recognises
her protector in the old servant, fondles around
him in the joy of buoyant life, and breathes her
last prayer for his liberty, is not there. Has he
given us the amiable traits of life thus drawn in
the substance of character ? The reader will say,
No ! And yet, strange as it may seem, he has
ridiculed Mrs. Stowe for the closing scenes of her
book, and in his concluding scenes of the " Golden
Christmas" is the most singular transposition ever
presented for the reader's mind.

Norman Morris is a different work; written
and intended for the stage. The work opens a
wide field for criticism, and our space, not allowing us to review it in detail, we will deal gently
with Mr. Simms, by assuring him that it never

will reach the stage unless it be remodled, both
in language and appointment.   The hero must be
a hero in language, and character, and soul; and
Clarissa must have words to give her inward sentiment pathos, refinement, and a spirit to play the
lady.   Speeches must be reduced, the language
of deep thought substituted for that of common
place, and the call-boy's language made to contrast with the hero's.   We have done with our
comparisons for the present.

   With regard to the careless amiability of Marie
St. Clare's character, Mr. Simms points us to
New England for specimens.   We have no desire
to charge want of energy and enterprise against
Southern ladies—far from it!   But there is something established in national opinion which is
hard to reason against; and even Southerners, we
mean the gentlemen, really admire it when they
come North and see the ladies.   It would be well
for Mr. Simms to open his views to a wider scene
of generality—leave the picture of that luxuriant-
living lady at the South, who would seem not born
to herself, but to some dependent existence; and
that there were *creatures* springing up around
her to be her handmaids for ever.   Go into New

England, see the energy, force of character,
moral industry, position, and happiness of the
working class; the distribution of property and
reigning cheerfulness and justice guiding her on
to a higher destiny—contrast it with the bloated
decline of dissolute life that surrounds him, and
from that contrast learn lessons of true republican
nobility.

Mrs. Stowe's book is like a faltering moon
hovering over his own city to light up the dark
scenes of horror and injustice. Let it be the
opening of a better prospect for the enslaved—
like a speck opening among the clouds to let down
the light of heaven for those who cry in need.
Let his thoughts be possessions for the benefit of
men, and truth in concord with his style of imper-
sonation. He must not be like Garrick, trembling
at his own bursts of passion; nor like Walpole,
standing in cold reluctant wonder. He must
be a Whitefield in voice and spirit, and a John
Howard in mind and energy—exploring the paths
that lead amid benighted nature, pointing to
the skirting precipice that may lead down into
the dark abyss.

In conclusion let us say to Mr. Simms, Think

no more of bold strokes and brilliant surprises; let your thoughts and actions merge into the stream of humanity, and go among simple nature and be its guardian. And in answer to your concluding text—to which you have referred Mrs. Stowe, " Thou shalt not bear false witness against thy neighbour"—let us say : BEAR FALSE WITNESS AGAINST THYSELF NO MORE.

NOTE.—This Review, with the exception of one or two pages at the commencement, was written in December last—since then the prediction with regard to the case of Craig has been verified : he was "honourably acquitted," but a man, if such he may be called, has really been hanged in South Carolina for killing his slave, eight years old. A friend, a true Southerner, writes us that he bore a general bad character; was a bad neighbour, and cruel to his family and slaves; that the evidence was stronger that he killed the mother of the child, than the child for whose death he paid the sad penalty; that he chained the little girl to a horse in the field, and whipped her severely, but that she was not under punishment when she died.

We know our informant to be a man of noble parts, yet a good and faithful secessionist; and he adds, that the coroner's jury having slurred the matter over, that circumstance influenced the jury that tried him. He wishes us to publish the circumstance, because he thinks it reflects great credit upon slave-holders; adding, that "he died firm, expecting reprieve or *rescue* to the last moment."